60 High Interest - Low Level
Science of Reading Comprehension and
Fluency Passages For Older
Emerging Readers

02   03   07

© Two Pencils and a Book.

ISBN: 979-8336936391

Information: https://www.teacherspayteachers.com/Store/Two-Pencils-And-A-Book

Table of Contents

Science of Reading and Fluency Research

To be considered "on level" in reading fluency, students should be able to read aloud an unrehearsed passage, (i.e., either narrative or expository, fiction or non-fiction that is 200 to 300 words in length) from a grade-level text, with at least 95% accuracy in word reading. As students read aloud, their reading should sound as effortless as if they were speaking (Hasbrouck & Glaser, 2012.) This does not come easily for some students, which is why fluency practice is so essential.

In order to be considered fluent readers, students in grades 9 through 12 should be able to correctly read 150 words per minute (Hasbrouck & Tindal, 2006). In 2006 and again in 2010, Hasbrouck and Hasbrouck & Tindal (respectively) put forth that "[i]t is sufficient for students to read unpracticed, grade-level text at the 50th percentile of oral reading fluency norms" and that "...teachers do not need to have students read faster because there is no evidence that reading faster than the 50th percentile increases comprehension." See chart below.

The best strategy for developing and improving reading fluency is to provide students with many opportunities to read the same passages orally several times. These exercises provide such opportunities. On each passage, there is space for reading fluency calculations. The best part is that the passages are quick and make it easy for students to read aloud repeatedly – and often – without taking up a lot of valuable classroom time. The activities can also be spread over several days.

This is an evidence-based program, and it works. Begin each passage as a guided reading. This is an evidence-based strategy for improving reading fluency. The student is asked to read the same passage three to five times, receiving feedback each time from the instructor or peer reviewer. Since this program is peer-to-peer, feedback comes from peers. By providing feedback on accuracy, rate and expression, students can incorporate those changes into each subsequent reading, eventually reaching a point of fluency with that particular passage. They can then move on to more difficult assignments.

Repeated readings of text can also contribute to better comprehension, one of the cornerstones of reading throughout life. All schools, from elementary to college, can easily provide students with repeated readings as well as paired passages of the same theme or topic.

For those teachers who want to mix-up full-class fluency lessons, one option is fluency-oriented reading instruction (FORI). This evidence-based practice begins with a teacher reading a particular passage aloud while students follow along in silent reading. Then, students read the passage aloud numerous times throughout the week, including echo, choral and partner reading. They also practice the passage for 15-30 minutes daily. At the end of a week, students engage in discussion, writing an essay or performing other activities that prove comprehension of the passage.

Grade	Percentile	Fall WPM	Winter WPM	Spring WPM
1	90		81	111
	75		47	82
	50		23	53
	25		12	28
	10		6	15
2	90	106	125	142
	75	79	100	117
	50	51	72	89
	25	25	42	61
	10	11	18	31
3	90	128	146	162
	75	99	120	137
	50	71	92	107
	25	44	62	78
	10	21	36	48
4	90	145	166	180
	75	119	139	152
	50	94	112	123
	25	68	87	98
	10	45	61	72

Grade	Percentile	Fall WPM	Winter WPM	Spring WPM
5	90	166	182	194
	75	139	156	168
	50	110	127	139
	25	85	99	109
	10	61	74	83
6	90	177	195	204
	75	153	167	177
	50	127	140	150
	25	98	111	122
	10	68	82	93
7	90	180	192	202
	75	156	165	177
	50	128	136	150
	25	102	109	123
	10	79	88	98
8	90	185	199	199
	75	161	173	177
	50	133	146	151
	25	106	115	125
	10	77	84	97

These passages are designed for older students who are very low readers.

If you are using this program with more than one student – partner up. Partnering students is engaging and lets everyone participate. Working with peers builds confidence and reinforces learning; additionally, by reading, tracking and reading again, student exposure to each passage is maximized. Research suggests that pairing readings with like-level reading partners is motivating and increases reading success.

Instruction for Group, Whole Class, or Zoom Fluency Practice

Before you begin, have a copy of one passage for each student. The PDF can be displayed before the whole class on a Smartboard or printed and projected on a document camera. As you explain the lessons, demonstrate what students will be doing.

Explain what fluency is - the rate and ease at which we read along with the flow of reading.

Break students into pairs and hand out one copy per student. If you are working with a group of students with varying abilities - pair like-leveled students together.

Explain the entire activity, as well as how to calculate combined words per minute, or CWPM. Then read the passage aloud. Have students track on their sheets as you read aloud. It is extremely beneficial for struggling students to hear the passage before they read it aloud. The goal isn't to have students stumble, but to optimize opportunities for ultimate success.

The first few times you do fluency as a class – the script below may be helpful:

1. **Check to make sure each person is in the right spot and then read the passage.**
2. **After you read the selected passage aloud, partner students and say something like:** *Put your name on your paper. Since you need to be marking your partner's paper, switch papers now. Raise your hand if you are Partner 1.*
3. **Pause until one student from each pair has their hand raised – acknowledge students when one person of each pair has their hand raised.**
4. **Raise your hand if you are Partner 2.** Pause until the other student from each pair has their hand raised – acknowledge students when the other partner has their hand raised.

   Excellent. When I say "Begin", all Partner 1s should quietly begin to read to their partners.

   All Partner 2s will use their pencils to keep track of their partner's errors. Partner 2s will put a line over each word pronounced incorrectly.

   When the timer goes off, all Partner 2s will circle the last word read, but Partner 1s will keep reading until the passage is complete. Does anyone have any questions?

5. **Set the timer for two minutes. If there are no questions -** *Begin.*
6. **When the timer goes off:** *Partner 2s, please mark your partner's score and give feedback to Partner 1s.*
7. **Walk around the room to make sure scores are being marked correctly.**
8. **Make sure students are ready and then switch for Partner 2s to read.**

   Ready? Begin.

Reading Levels

Hamzah the Fantastic TikTok Star
ATOS Level: 4.2
Word Count: 225
Average Word Length: 4.2
Average Sentence Length: 8
Average Vocabulary Level: 3.1
Reading Level: Grade Level 2-3

Billie Eilish
ATOS Level: 3.9
Word Count: 240
Average Word Length: 4.2
Average Sentence Length: 8.3
Average Vocabulary Level: 2.7
Reading Level: Grade Level 2-3

Kinds of Popular
ATOS Level: 2.9
Word Count: 242
Average Word Length: 4.1
Average Sentence Length: 6.2
Average Vocabulary Level: 2.6
Reading Level: Grade Level 1-2

Six Flags Magic Mountain
ATOS Level: 4.7
Word Count: 253
Average Word Length: 4.2
Average Sentence Length: 9
Average Vocabulary Level: 2.6
Reading Level: Grade Level 3

Soccer's Cristiano Ronaldo
TOS Level: 4.4
Word Count: 250
Average Word Length: 4
Average Sentence Length: 9.3
Average Vocabulary Level: 2.6
Reading Level: Grade Level 3

Sadie Sink – Actress
ATOS Level: 3.4
Word Count: 191
Average Word Length: 4.3
Average Sentence Length: 7.3
Average Vocabulary Level: 2.6
Reading Level: Grade Level 2-3

My Bucket List
ATOS Level: 2.2
Word Count: 235
Average Word Length: 3.9
Average Sentence Length: 6.2
Average Vocabulary Level: 2.1
Reading Level: Grade Level 1-2

YouTube Videos
ATOS Level: 4.0
Word Count: 225
Average Word Length: 4
Average Sentence Length: 8.7
Average Vocabulary Level:2.3
Reading Level: Grade Level 2-3

The Cell Phone Revolution
ATOS Level: 6.9
Word Count: 240
Average Word Length: 4.4
Average Sentence Length: 12.6
Average Vocabulary Level: 3.1
Reading Level: Grade Level 4-5

Fantasy Football
ATOS Level: 5.2
Word Count: 222
Average Word Length: 4.2
Average Sentence Length: 9.2
Average Vocabulary Level: 3.2
Reading Level: Grade Level 3-4

Not Your Parent's Video Game
ATOS Level: 4.6
Word Count: 204
Average Word Length: 4.5
Average Sentence Length: 8.5
Average Vocabulary Level: 3.1
Reading Level: Grade Level 2-3

Things to Do Before College
ATOS Level: 4.1
Word Count: 199
Average Word Length: 4.2
Average Sentence Length: 8.3
Average Vocabulary Level: 2.8
Reading Level: Grades 3-4

National Go Skateboarding Day
ATOS Level: 3.8
Word Count: 255
Average Word Length: 3.9
Average Sentence Length: 8.8
Average Vocabulary Level: 2.5
Reading Level: Grade Level 2-3

Skateboarding Heroes
ATOS Level: 4.0
Word Count: 226
Average Word Length: 4.3
Average Sentence Length: 7.8
Average Vocabulary Level: 2.9
Reading Level: Grade Level 2-3

National Pizza Day
TOS Level: 4.6
Word Count: 193
Average Word Length: 4.2
Average Sentence Length: 8.5
Average Vocabulary Level: 2.9
Reading Level: Grades 3-4

Music
ATOS Level: 3.4
Word Count: 266
Average Word Length: 3.9
Average Sentence Length: 7
Average Vocabulary Level: 2.9
Reading Level: Grade Level 2-3

Rapper Young Thug
ATOS Level: 4.3
Word Count: 259
Average Word Length: 4.1
Average Sentence Length: 7.6
Average Vocabulary Level: 3.3
Grade Level 3

Kanye West
ATOS Level: 3.4
Word Count: 224
Average Word Length: 4.1
Average Sentence Length: 6.8
Average Vocabulary Level: 2.9
Grade Level 2-3

Cardi B
ATOS Level: 5.2
Word Count: 216
Average Word Length: 4
Average Sentence Length: 9.4
Average Vocabulary Level: 3.4
Grade Level 3-4

Emma Watson
ATOS Level: 4.6
Word Count: 186
Average Word Length: 4.3
Average Sentence Length: 8.5
Average Vocabulary Level: 3.2
Grade Level 3

Minecraft
ATOS Level: 2.9
Word Count: 177
Average Word Length: 4.6
Average Sentence Length: 6.8
Average Vocabulary Level: 3.2
Reading Level: Grade 3

Sheila Johnson
ATOS Level: 5.4
Word Count: 211
Average Word Length: 4.6
Average Sentence Length: 9.2
Average Vocabulary Level: 3.2
Reading Level: Grade 3.7

Sophia Bush
ATOS Level: 3.9
Word Count: 251
Average Word Length: 4
Average Sentence Length: 8.4
Average Vocabulary Level: 2.8
Reading Level: Grade 3

Chadwick Boseman
ATOS Level:
5.1 Word Count: 211
Average Word Length: 4.4
Average Sentence Length: 8.8
Average Vocabulary Level: 3.2
Reading Level: Grade 3.8

Black Panther: Marvel Comics
ATOS Level: 5.1
Word Count: 191
Average Word Length: 4.7
Average Sentence Length: 8.7
Average Vocabulary Level: 3.4
Reading Level: Grade 3

Spider-Man
ATOS Level: 5.2
Word Count: 222
Average Word Length: 4.3
Average Sentence Length: 8.9
Average Vocabulary Level: 3.5
Reading Level Grade 4

Katniss Everdeen
ATOS Level: 3.3
Word Count: 222
Average Word Length: 4.3
Average Sentence Length: 6.3
Average Vocabulary Level: 3.2
Reading Level: Grade 2

Victoria Roth
ATOS Level: 5.5
Word Count: 210
Average Word Length: 4.4
Average Sentence Length: 9.1
Average Vocabulary Level: 3.5
Reading Level: Grade 4

Danny Duncan
ATOS Level: 4.8
Word Count: 218
Average Word Length: 4.1
Average Sentence Length: 9.5
Average Vocabulary Level: 2.8
Reading Level Grade 3

Emma Chamberlain
ATOS Level: 5
Word Count: 242
Average Word Length: 4.5
Average Sentence Length: 9.7
Average Vocabulary Level: 3.8
Reading Level: Grade 5

Nike Air Force 1
ATOS Level: 2.9
Word Count: 202
Average Word Length: 4.2
Average Sentence Length: 7.2
Average Vocabulary Level: 2.1
Reading Level: Grade 2

LeBron James
ATOS Level: 5.4
Word Count: 223
Average Word Length: 4.2
Average Sentence Length: 10.1
Average Vocabulary Level: 3.1
Reading Level: Grade 4

Joan of Arc Part I
ATOS Level: 4.3
Word Count: 256
Average Word Length: 4.1
Average Sentence Length: 8.5
Average Vocabulary Level: 2.9
Reading Level: Grade 3

Joan of Arc: Part II
ATOS Level: 3.9
Word Count: 196
Average Word Length: 4.2
Average Sentence Length: 8.2
Average Vocabulary Level: 2.7
Reading Level: Grade 2

Wonder Woman
ATOS Level: 5.3
Word Count: 179
Average Word Length: 4.6
Average Sentence Length: 9
Average Vocabulary Level: 3.6
Reading Level: Grade 3

Magic the Gathering
ATOS Level: 5.5
Word Count: 230
Average Word Length: 4.7
Average Sentence Length: 8.5
Average Vocabulary Level: 3.9
Reading Level: Grade 4

Six Flags
ATOS Level: 4.7
Word Count: 269
Average Word Length: 4.4
Average Sentence Length: 9.3
Average Vocabulary Level: 2.9
Reading Level: Grade 3

Wakeboarding
ATOS Level: 5.8
Word Count: 250
Average Word Length: 4.6
Average Sentence Length: 10.4
Average Vocabulary Level: 3.3
Reading Level: Grade 4

Where the Wild Things Are
ATOS Level: 4.0
Word Count: 276
Average Word Length: 3.8
Average Sentence Length: 11.3
Average Vocabulary Level: 1.7
Reading Level: Grade 2

Random Facts
ATOS Level: 5.0
Word Count: 273
Average Word Length: 4.2
Average Sentence Length: 10.5
Average Vocabulary Level: 2.7
Reading Level: Grade 3

Sky Brown
ATOS Level: 3.3
Word Count: 141
Average Word Length: 4.2
Average Sentence Length: 6.4
Average Vocabulary Level: 3.1
Reading Level: Grade 2

Apple Watch
ATOS Level: 2.3
Word Count: 180
Average Word Length: 3.6
Average Sentence Length: 5.8
Average Vocabulary Level: 3.1
Reading Level: Grade 2

Busch Gardens
ATOS Level: 3.0
Word Count: 180
Average Word Length: 3.9
Average Sentence Length: 6.9
Average Vocabulary Level: 2.8
Reading Level: Grade 2

Water Country USA
TOS Level: 2.9
Word Count: 209
Average Word Length: 4.1
Average Sentence Length: 7.2
Average Vocabulary Level: 2.5
Reading Level: Grade 3

Rhythmic Gymnastics
ATOS Level: 3.8
Word Count: 150
Average Word Length: 4.2
Average Sentence Length: 6.8
Average Vocabulary Level: 3.2
Reading Level: Grade 3

Extreme Fire Behavior
ATOS Level: 2.0
Word Count: 173
Average Word Length: 3.9
Average Sentence Length: 5.8
Average Vocabulary Level: 2.2
Reading Level: Grades 2-3

What Happened to Abbie
ATOS Level: 1.4
Word Count: 179
Average Word Length: 4.1
Average Sentence Length: 5.3
Average Vocabulary Level: 1.9
Reading Level: Grades 1-2

Abbie Part 2
ATOS Level: 1.0
Word Count: 197
Average Word Length: 3.9
Average Sentence Length: 4.9
Average Vocabulary Level: 1.5
Reading Level: Grades 1-2

Chinese Kidnapping
ATOS Level: 2.2
Word Count: 226
Average Word Length: 3.8
Average Sentence Length: 6.8
Average Vocabulary Level: 1.9
Reading Level: Grade 2

Fact or Opinion: Snicker Bar Candy
ATOS Level: 3.8
Word Count: 141
Average Word Length: 4.3
Average Sentence Length: 6.1
Average Vocabulary Level: 2.8
Reading Level: Grades 2-3

Sharks
ATOS Level: 2.4
Word Count: 118
Average Word Length: 4.3
Average Sentence Length: 5.6
Average Vocabulary Level: 2.3
Reading Level: Grade 2

Lions
ATOS Level: 2.9
Word Count: 183
Average Word Length: 4.1
Average Sentence Length: 6.8
Average Vocabulary Level: 2.3
Reading Level: Grade 2

80s Fashion
ATOS Level: 2.5
Word Count: 195
Average Word Length: 4.1
Average Sentence Length: 4.8
Average Vocabulary Level: 2.9
Reading Level: Grades 1-2

Extreme Fire
ATOS Level: 4.5
Word Count: 48
Average Word Length: 4.3
Average Sentence Length: 9.6
Average Vocabulary Level: 2.7
Reading Level: Grade 3

Jesse James
ATOS Level: 2.9
Word Count: 160
Average Word Length: 4.1
Average Sentence Length: 5.7
Average Vocabulary Level: 3
Reading Level: Grade 3

Sam Bass - Outlaw
ATOS Level: 2.5
Word Count: 197
Average Word Length: 3.8
Average Sentence Length: 5.8
Average Vocabulary Level: 2.4
Reading Level: Grade 2

Jack the Ripper - Serial Killer
ATOS Level: 2.4
Word Count: 173
Average Word Length: 3.9
Average Sentence Length: 6
Average Vocabulary Level: 2.4
Reading Level: Grade 2

The Panama Canal
ATOS Level: 3.1
Word Count: 250
Average Word Length: 3.8
Average Sentence Length: 7.1
Average Vocabulary Level: 2.4
Reading Level: Grades 2-3

Rap
ATOS Level: 3.2
Word Count: 147
Average Word Length: 4.3
Average Sentence Length: 6.1
Average Vocabulary Level: 2.8
Reading Levels: Grades 2-3

Mars
ATOS Level: 2.1
Word Count: 127
Average Word Length: 3.9
Average Sentence Length: 5.8
Average Vocabulary Level: 2.1
Reading Levels: Grades 1-2

Hamzah the Fantastic
TICTOK STAR

Hamzah the Fantastic is a TikTok star. His birthday is March 5, 2002. Hamzah makes funny videos. His videos often have pranks in them. They are made from his point of view. Point of View, or POV, shots are when social media stars pretend to be someone - like your boyfriend or your best friend. Hamzah's videos are very popular.

Hamzah has over 1.6 million fans. He has 1.6 million fans and has only been on TikTok since 2019. He has over 44.5 million likes. On TikTok, Hamzah is part of the **FreakShow** group. Other members of the group are Claire Drake and Chase Rutherford.

Hamzah is also on Instagram, but he doesn't post there often. Even so, he has over 600,000 followers on the platform.

Hamzah has a little brother. His brother appears on his TikToks. Not much is known about his parents.

Hamzah created a diss track with Freddie Dread. It is called **6 Feet**. Hamzah made the track to diss his friends. Why? The **FreakShow** group recorded a track without him. He was in Canada. COVID meant they couldn't get together. He got back at them by making a song of his own. His song, or track, is full of inside jokes. The track is full of inside jokes aimed at his friends. The title **6 Feet** is a COVID reference.

Have you ever seen TikTok star Hamzah the Fantastic?

Directions: Please select the best response.

1. Members of the **FreakShow** group include:
   - a.   Claire Drake
   - b.   Chase Rutherford
   - c.   Hamzah the Fantastic.
   - d.   all of the above.
   - e.   none of the above.

2. How many Instagram followers does Hamzah have?
   - a.   1.6 million
   - b.   6
   - c.   6 million
   - d.   600,000

3. The track **6 Feet** is about
   - a.   Hamzah's friends.
   - b.   COVID.
   - c.   a diss track because he could not be in a song because of COVID.
   - d.   not enough information to tell.

4. Hamzah's videos are from
   - a.   a POV.
   - b.   the USA.
   - c.   a diss track.
   - d.   Instagram.

Name: _____

Hamzah the Fantastic - TICTOK STAR

Hamzah the Fantastic is a TikTok star. His birthday is March 5, 2002. Hamzah	14
makes funny videos. His videos often have pranks in them. They are made from	28
his point of view. Point of View, or POV, shots are when social media stars	43
pretend to be someone – like your boyfriend or your best friend. Hamzah's	55
videos are very popular.	59
Hamzah has over 1.6 million fans. He has 1.6 million fans and has only been	74
on TikTok since 2019. He has over 44.5 million likes. On TikTok, Hamzah is part	89
of the FreakShow group. Other members of the group are Claire Drake and	102
Chase Rutherford.	104
Hamzah is also on Instagram, but he doesn't post there often. Even so, he	118
has over 600,000 followers on the platform.	125
Hamzah has a little brother. His brother appears on his TikToks. Not much is	139
known about his parents.	143
Hamzah created a diss track with Freddie Dread. It is called 6 Feet. Hamzah	158
made the track to diss his friends. Why? The FreakShow group recorded a	171
track without him. He was in Canada. COVID meant they couldn't get together.	184
He got back at them by making a song of his own. His song, or track, is full of	203
inside jokes. The track is full of inside jokes aimed at his friends. The title 6 Feet	220
is a COVID reference.	224
Have you ever seen TikTok star Hamzah the Fantastic?	233

Words Read:	Words Read:	Words Read:
minus mistakes:	minus mistakes:	minus mistakes:
equals wpms:	equals wpms:	equals wpms:

Name: _____

Billie Eilish
SINGER & SONGWRITER

Billie Eilish is a singer. She is also a songwriter. Billie was born in Los Angeles, California. Her single, "Ocean Eyes" went viral. It has over 1.5 billion streams on Spotify. The song was later released by Interscope Records.

Billie's first studio album is *When We All Fall Asleep*. It was one of the best-selling albums of 2019.

Billie's won five Grammy's. She's won two American Music Awards. She's also won three MTV Awards. Billie is the youngest person to be up for the four main Grammys in the same year. The four main Grammys are Best New Artist, Record of the Year, Song of the Year and Album of the Year.

Billie is the 23rd biggest singer of the digital singles era. She has sold more than 40 million singles. And that is only in the U.S.

Billie was homeschooled. Her mother was her teacher. Her mother also taught Billie how to write songs. Billie wrote her first song at age 11. Her parents told her she could do anything she wanted – even be a music superstar.

Billie is more than a music superstar. She fights for animal rights. She is a vegan. She does not wear wool. She does not use dairy. She won a PETA award for her work helping animals.

Billie Eilish was famous at a young age. That means nothing to her. She is unstoppable. With a great voice and a big heart – she is taking the world by storm.

Directions: Please select the best response.

1. Billie wrote her first album at age
   a.   11.
   b.   23.
   c.   40.
   d.   12.

2. Billie was the youngest to be named
   a.   in the top four MTV Award categories
   b.   in the top four Grammy categories
   c.   Artist of the Year
   d.   Writer of the Year

3.   Why is the digital music era special for Billie?
   a.   She is a vegan.
   b.   She produces videos.
   c.   She has sold more than 40 million singles.
   d.   not enough information to tell.

4.   Billie fights for _____ rights.
   a.   singer
   b.   writer
   c.   animal
   d.   activist

Name: _____

Billie Eilish – SINGER & SONGWRITER

Billie Eilish is a singer. She is also a songwriter. Billie was born in Los Angeles,	16
California. Her single, "Ocean Eyes" went viral. It has over 1.5 billion streams on	30
Spotify. The song was later released by Interscope Records.	39

Billie's first studio album is *When We All Fall Asleep*. It was one of the best-selling   66
albums of 2019.   59

Billie's won five Grammy's. She's won two American Music Awards. She's also won   72
three MTV Awards. Billie is the youngest person to be up for the four main Grammys in   89
the same year. The four main Grammys are Best New Artist, Record of the Year, Song   105
of the Year and Album of the Year.   113

Billie is the 23rd biggest singer of the digital singles era. She has sold more than 40   130
million singles. And that is only in the U.S.   139

Billie was homeschooled. Her mother was her teacher. Her mother also taught   151
Billie how to write songs. Billie wrote her first song at age 11. Her parents told her she   168
could do anything she wanted – even be a music superstar.   178

Billie is more than a music superstar. She fights for animal rights. She is a vegan.   194
She does not wear wool. She does not use dairy. She won a PETA award for her work   212
helping animals.   214

Billie Eilish was famous at a young age. That means nothing to her. She is   229
unstoppable. With a great voice and a big heart – she is taking the world by storm.   245

Words Read:	Words Read:	Words Read:
minus mistakes:	minus mistakes:	minus mistakes:
equals wpms:	equals wpms:	equals wpms:

Kinds of Popular

There is that one group. Maybe you are in it. The popular kids. The kids who seem to have it all. Some are nice. Some are, well, not-so-nice. Some are great people. Some are bullies.

Being popular. It matters so much - at least when you are in school. Popular. What does it mean? Why does it matter? Why do we care so much?

Popularity. Some people are popular because they are likable. Some are popular because of reputation.

There is more than one way to be popular. A study says there are three ways. The study says there are three types of teen popularity. The study also says that being popular is not the same as being liked.

The first type of popular teen is aggressive. Mean Girls come to mind. Popularity by bullying. This is not a great way to be popular.

The second type is through cooperation. Being nice. Getting along. This group is well-liked and well-adjusted.

The third type is a bit of both. It is a blend of the first two. These people are aggressive but then are nice after they hurt your feelings. They do things on purpose. They are very tricky. They use a bit of both to keep their popularity. This group of teens are the *most* popular people.

How many popular people do you know? What type of popular do you think they are? Or maybe that popular person is you?

Directions: Please select the best response.

1. There are _____ types of being popular.
   - a. 3
   - b. 2
   - c. 7
   - d. 12

2. Bullies fall into the
   - a. nice type of popularity.
   - b. bullying type of popularity.
   - c. the aggressive type of popularity.
   - d. loser type – bullies are never popular.

3. Popularity through cooperation means popular kids
   - a. stop bullies.
   - b. are mean girls.
   - c. try to get along.
   - d. are feared

4. "There is more than _____ way to be popular"
   - a. six
   - b. two
   - c. one
   - d. 12

5. Summarize the passage:

_____

_____

_____

_____

Name: _____

Kinds of Popular

There is that one group. Maybe you are in it. The popular kids. The kids who seem to	18
have it all. Some are nice. Some are, well, not-so-nice. Some are great people. Some	35
are bullies.	37
Being popular. It matters so much – at least when you are in school. Popular. What	52
does it mean? Why does it matter? Why do we care so much?	65
Popularity. Some people are popular because they are likable. Some are popular	77
because of reputation.	80
There is more than one way to be popular. A study says there are three ways. The	97
study says there are three types of teen popularity. The study also says that being	112
popular is not the same as being liked.	120
The first type of popular teen is aggressive. Mean Girls come to mind. Popularity by	135
bullying. This is not a great way to be popular.	145
The second type is through cooperation. Being nice. Getting along. This group is	158
well-liked and well-adjusted.	163
The third type is a bit of both. It is a blend of the first two. These people are	182
aggressive but then are nice after they hurt your feelings. They do things on purpose.	197
They are very tricky. They use a bit of both to keep their popularity. This group of	214
teens are the *most* popular people.	220
How many popular people do you know? What type of popular do you think they	235
are? Or maybe that popular person is you?	243

Words Read:	Words Read:	Words Read:
minus mistakes:	minus mistakes:	minus mistakes:
equals wpms:	equals wpms:	equals wpms:

Six Flags Magic Mountain

It sits on a hill in Valencia, California. When you are on I-5 from Los Angeles north – it appears. Giant steel tracks against the blue of the sky. The steel shoots up, up, up. It seems to touch the sun. The closer to the park you get – the bigger they become. What are they? They are the 19 roller coasters of Six Flags Magic Mountain.

Magic Mountain has 19 roller coasters. That is a world record. Over 3.5 million people visit the park each year. That is a lot of roller coaster riding.

The park opened in 1971. It had 33 attractions. Many of the rides and attractions were built by the same people who built the first rides at Disneyland.

In 1976, the park went through major changes. Magic Mountain became the first park in the world to have a 360-degree steel looping coaster.

In 1978, *Colossus* was added. At the time, Colossus was the fastest and longest wooden roller coaster in the world. Colossus closed after one year. It reopened as a much better ride.

In 1979, the park sold to Six Flags and roller coasters seemed to grow like seeds.

There are 11 themed area in the park. Each area has its own rides, attractions and food. Of the 19 roller coasters – 13 are considered extreme. An extreme coaster is not for the weak at heart.

If you love roller coasters and are ever near Los Angeles – hop on over to Magic Mountain. You will not be disappointed.

1. How many roller coasters are at Magic Mountain?
   a.   13
   b.   19
   c.   33
   d.   11

2. In 1976, the park opened the first
   a.   roller coaster in the world.
   b.   steel roller coaster in the world.
   c.   the first 360-degree loop roller coaster.
   d.   Colossus.

3.   The park has _____ themed areas.
   a.   13
   b.   19
   c.   33
   d.   11

4.. Magic Mountain is located
   a.   in Los Angeles
   b.   in Valencia
   c.   in Disneyland
   d.   in Texas

5. Colossus is
   a. a wooden coaster
   b. a steel coaster
   c. a looped coaster
   d. a tropical drink

Six Flags Magic Mountain

It sits on a hill in Valencia, California. When you are on I-5 from Los Angeles north | 18
– it appears. Giant steel tracks against the blue of the sky. The steel shoots up, up, up. | 35
It seems to touch the sun. The closer to the park you get – the bigger they become. | 52
What are they? They are the 19 roller coasters of Six Flags Magic Mountain. | 66

Magic Mountain has 19 roller coasters. That is a world record. Over 3.5 million | 80
people visit the park each year. That is a lot of roller coaster riding. | 94

The park opened in 1971. It had 33 attractions. Many of the rides and attractions | 109
were built by the same people who built the first rides at Disneyland. | 122

In 1976, the park went through major changes. Magic Mountain became the first | 135
park in the world to have a 360-degree steel looping coaster. | 147

In 1978, *Colossus* was added. At the time, Colossus was the fastest and longest | 161
wooden roller coaster in the world. Colossus closed after one year. It reopened as a | 176
much better ride. | 179

In 1979, the park sold to Six Flags and roller coasters seemed to grow like seeds. | 195

There are 11 themed area in the park. Each area has its own rides, attractions and | 211
food. Of the 19 roller coasters – 13 are considered extreme. An extreme coaster is not | 226
for the weak at heart. | 231

If you love roller coasters and are ever near Los Angeles – hop on over to Magic | 247
Mountain. You will not be disappointed. | 253

Words Read:	Words Read:	Words Read:
minus mistakes:	minus mistakes:	minus mistakes:
equals wpms:	equals wpms:	equals wpms:

Name: _____

Soccer's Cristiano Ronaldo

Cristiano Ronaldo (CR) is the most popular soccer player in the world. Some say he is the most popular sports star in the world.

CR is from Portugal. He has played pro soccer since 2003. He was only 18 when he signed his first contract. Since then, CR has become his country's highest goal maker. He has also been ranked as the world's highest paid athlete for the years 2016 and 2017.

Today, CR makes about $109 million per year. That is a lot of money. He is the first soccer player to be a billionaire. That is billion with a **B**. That's a lot of money to kick a ball around.

CR did not always have it easy. He grew up poor. He is the youngest of four children. He has one older brother. He has two older sisters. They all shared a room growing up.

CR began playing semi-pro soccer at age 14.

A short time later, he had to quit soccer due to a heart condition. He had heart surgery as a teen, went back to the field and made history – and millions.

Not only is CR rich and great looking – he is the most followed person on Instagram. He has over 636 million followers. Leo Mess is next with 550 million. Get this – for every sponsored post on his Instagram – CR makes 1 million dollars.

He believes in hard work and cooperation. CR believes those two things have carried him far. I think he is right.

1. CR makes $109 million a year. He is a
   - a.   millionaire.
   - b.   a premiere US soccer player.
   - c.   a billionaire.
   - d.   the oldest of four children.

2. When CR was young, he
   - a.   hated soccer.
   - b.   was poor.
   - c.   lived in a middle-class neighborhood.
   - d.   had two brothers.

3. CR began to play semi-pro soccer
   - a.   in 2003.
   - b.   in 2013.
   - c.   at age 14.
   - d.   in 2017.

4. How many Instagram followers does CR have?
   - a.   about 244
   - b.   about 660
   - c.   about 1 million
   - d.   about 109 million

5. In 2016, CR was
   - a.   ranked the number one soccer player in the world.
   - b.   the highest paid athlete in the world.
   - c.   living with his three siblings

Name: _____

Soccer's Cristiano Ronaldo

Cristiano Ronaldo (CR) is the most popular soccer player in the world. Some say	14
he is the most popular sports star in the world.	24
CR is from Portugal. He has played pro soccer since 2003. He was only 18 when he	41
signed his first contract. Since then, CR has become his country's highest goal maker.	55
He has also been ranked as the world's highest paid athlete for the years 2016 and	71
2017.	72
Today, CR makes about $109 million per year. That is a lot of money. He is the first	90
soccer player to be a billionaire. That is billion with a B. That's a lot of money to kick a	110
ball around.	112
CR did not always have it easy. He grew up poor. He is the youngest of four	129
children. He has one older brother. He has two older sisters. They all shared a room	145
growing up.	147
CR began playing semi-pro soccer at age 14.	156
A short time later, he had to quit soccer due to a heart condition. He had heart	173
surgery as a teen, went back to the field and made history – and millions.	187
Not only is CR rich and great looking – he is the most followed person on	202
Instagram. He has over 636 million followers. Leo Mess is next with 550 million. Get this	218
– for every sponsored post on his Instagram – CR makes 1 million dollars.	230
He believes in hard work and cooperation. CR believes those two things have	243
carried him far. I think he is right.	251

Words Read:	Words Read:	Words Read:
minus mistakes:	minus mistakes:	minus mistakes:
equals wpms:	equals wpms:	equals wpms:

Name: _____

Sadie Sink - Actress

Sadie Sink is an actress. She plays Max Mayfield on *Stranger Things*. *Stranger Things* is a series on Netflix.

Sadie was born on April 16, 2002, in Texas. In 2009, Sadie and her brother staged *High School Musical* for her parents. Her mother saw Sadie's talent. Her mother sent Sadie to acting school. Sadie also took voice and dance lessons.

Sadie's first acting gig was playing Duffy in *Annie* on Broadway. She also played the young Queen Elizabeth II. She played the young queen in a play. The play was called *The Audience*.

Sadie made about $150,000 per episode of *Stranger Things*. She played a tomboy. She was added to the show in season two. Her role went from small in season two to major in season three. She in the award-winning film "The Whale."

Sadie loves animals. She raises money and speaks out for animal rights. She is a vegan.

"I am a vegan for animals. It also helps the environment," Sadie's said.

Sadie also models. The first time she walked the catwalk was in 2018. It was in Paris. A catwalk is another name for runway.

Sadie has three older brothers and a younger sister.

1. Sadie and her brother staged
   a.   Stranger Things.
   b.   High School Musical.
   c.   Annie.
   d.   The Audience.

2. Sadie plays Max in
   a.   Stranger Things.
   b.   High School Musical.
   c.   Annie.
   d.   The Audience.

3. Sadie's speaks out for
   a.   Max.
   b.   the queen's rights.
   c.   veganism.
   d.   animals.

4. In season _____ of *Stranger Things* Sadie's role went from small to major.
   a.   Season 1
   b.   Season 2
   c.   Season 3
   d.   Season 4

5. Sadie
   a.   is an only child.
   b.   has three brothers and no sisters.
   c.   has a sister and three brothers.

Sadie Sink - Actress

Sadie Sink is an actress. She plays Max Mayfield on *Stranger Things. Stranger*	13
Things is a series on Netflix.	19
Sadie was born on April 16, 2002, in Texas. In 2009, Sadie and her brother staged	35
High School Musical for her parents. Her mother saw Sadie's talent. Her mother sent	49
Sadie to acting school. Sadie also took voice and dance lessons.	60
Sadie's first acting gig was playing Duffy in *Annie* on Broadway. She also played	74
the young Queen Elizabeth II. She played the young queen in a play. The play was	90
called *The Audience.*	93
Sadie made about $150,000 per episode of *Stranger Things.* She played a tomboy.	106
She was added to the show in season two. Her role went from small in season two to	224
major in season three. She in the award-winning film "The Whale."	236
Sadie loves animals. She raises money and speaks out for animal rights. She is a	251
vegan.	252
"I am a vegan for animals. It also helps the environment," Sadie's said.	265
Sadie also models. The first time she walked the catwalk was in 2018. It was in	281
Paris. A catwalk is another name for runway.	289
Sadie has three older brothers and a younger sister.	298

Words Read:	Words Read:	Words Read:
minus mistakes:	minus mistakes:	minus mistakes:
equals wpms:	equals wpms:	equals wpms:

My Bucket List

A bucket list is a list of things you want to do. Do you have a bucket list? You should. But where would you start? What would you have on your list? Here are some ideas.

Get a high score on a video game. A really high score. This will take skill. This will take luck. This may take a lot of time, but if you like gaming – shoot for a super high score.

Go wild with your hair. Once. Go blue. Go pink. Change the style. Do something different and edgy. Worried about having bright red hair until it grows out? Use hair chalk. It washes right out. Have fun with it.

Go 24 hours without television or the internet. Add music too. Go 24 hours without any tech. This one may not be easy. Think about it. Besides sleeping, when was the last time you went three hours without checking your phone or using technology?

Try a new food. Ever eaten frog's legs? How about sushi? Try something out of the norm. A great place to try fun foods is an Asian Market. You may even find your new favorite food there.

Sleep under the stars. There is nothing like looking up at the night sky on a clear night. It's a super sense of freedom.

There are so many things most of us have never done. What would be on your bucket list?

1. What is a bucket list?
   a. a list of new hair styles.
   b. a list of things to do.
   c. a list of things you want to do.
   d. a list of buckets.

2. The article mentions all of the following bucket list items but
   a. pink hair.
   b. bungee jumping.
   c. eating something new.
   d. go without your phone.

3. New foods the article suggest you try do not include
   a. sushi.
   b. frog's legs.
   c. something from an Asian market.
   d. alligator.

4. According to the article, sleeping under the stars can be
   a. cold.
   b. freeing.
   c. wild.
   d. wet.

5. Summarize the article.

_____

_____

_____

_____

_____

My Bucket List

A bucket list is a list of things you want to do. Do you have a bucket list? You	19
should. But where would you start? What would you have on your list? Here are some	35
ideas.	36
Get a high score on a video game. A really high score. This will take skill. This will	54
take luck. This may take a lot of time, but if you like gaming – shoot for a super high	73
score.	74
Go wild with your hair. Once. Go blue. Go pink. Change the style. Do something	89
different and edgy. Worried about having bright red hair until it grows out? Use hair	104
chalk. It washes right out. Have fun with it.	113
Go 24 hours without television or the internet. Add music too. Go 24 hours without	128
any tech. This one may not be easy. Think about it. Besides sleeping, when was the last	145
time you went three hours without checking your phone or using technology?	157
Try a new food. Ever eaten frog's legs? How about sushi? Try something out of the	173
norm. A great place to try fun foods is an Asian Market. You may even find your new	191
favorite food there.	194
Sleep under the stars. There is nothing like looking up at the night sky on a clear	211
night. It's a super sense of freedom.	218
There are so many things most of us have never done. What would be on your	234
bucket list?	236

Words Read:	Words Read:	Words Read:
minus mistakes:	minus mistakes:	minus mistakes:
equals wpms:	equals wpms:	equals wpms:

YouTube Videos

YouTube is the place to find new and hip videos. Wait? Is "hip" still a word? Is it still a thing? Anyway, if you want fresh and hot videos – YouTube is the place to go.

But what if it is you who wants to make videos? Where do you begin?

First, you need to know that making awesome videos may not be the way to YouTube success. What? It's true.

The most important thing is that people need to be able to find your video. This means giving it a great title. Make sure search engines can find it. If they can't find it, people can't see it. Use hashtags to help drive traffic. Once you get people to your videos - give them something they don't expect. Surprise them.

The second thing to do is make videos people want to watch. Look for topics people are interested in. The best videos to start with are "how to" videos. A recent study reports that 53% of people watch two or more "how to" videos per week. Per week!

The most important thing to do is to get started. If you want to make YouTube videos, make a video. If you want to make successful YouTube videos, pick up your phone and show people how to do something you're good at doing.

What are you waiting for?

1. The first thing the article says makes a video successful is
   a.   make awesome videos.
   b.   for people to be able to find your video.
   c.   select interesting topics.
   d.   use a lot of special effects.

2. The second thing to do is to
   a.   look for things people are interested in.
   b.   make videos you love.
   c.   buy a high-end video camera.
   d.   start a production company.

3. The best videos to start with are
   a.   music videos.
   b.   short films for festivals.
   c.   how to videos.
   d.   prank videos.

4. According to the article, hashtags are used to
   a.   help drive traffic.
   b.   form a production team.
   c.   help you film with your phone.
   d.   make your videos interesting.

5. Write a one sentence summary of article.

   _____

   _____

   _____

   _____

YouTube Videos

YouTube is the place to find new and hip videos. Wait? Is "hip" still a word? Is it still a thing? Anyway, if you want fresh and hot videos – YouTube is the place to go. | 18 / 36

But what if it is you who wants to make videos? Where do you begin? | 51

First, you need to know that making awesome videos may not be the way to YouTube success. What? It's true. | 66 / 71

The most important thing is that people need to be able to find your video. This means giving it a great title. Make sure search engines can find it. If they can't find it, people can't see it. Use hashtags to help drive traffic. Once you get people to your videos – give them something they don't expect. Surprise them. | 87 / 105 / 121 / 130

The second thing to do is make videos people want to watch. Look for topics people are interested in. The best videos to start with are "how to" videos. A recent study reports that 53% of people watch two or more "how to" videos per week. Per week! | 145 / 161 / 177 / 178

The most important thing to do is to get started. If you want to make YouTube videos, make a video. If you want to make successful YouTube videos, pick up your phone and show people how to do something you're good at doing. | 194 / 209 / 221

What are you waiting for? | 226

Words Read:	Words Read:	Words Read:
minus mistakes:	minus mistakes:	minus mistakes:
equals wpms:	equals wpms:	equals wpms:

Name: _____

The Cell Phone Revolution

A Pew Research study found that 53% of children in the U.S. get their first phone by age 11. A study by "Common Sense Media" found that 95% of U.S. teens have their own smart phone.

Seventy percent of those teens check social media several times per day. That is up from 34% in 2012. And half of all teens say their phones distract them from their homework. Their phones also distract them from the people they are with.

"Common Sense Media" also reported that teens spend 7 hours per day on their phones. Tweens spend nearly 5 hours on theirs. But that doesn't mean **real** hours? The study double counted multi-tasking, so what's the real number?

If a teen is texting a friend, streaming a video and is on social media for 10 minutes at one time – the study counted that as 30 minutes.

The study also pointed out that during those seven hours on their phones, teens were also doing chores, riding on buses, in cars, socializing, eating meals – doing just about everything else.

In sum, teens and their phones are joined. It is interesting to note that youth from families making $35,000 per year spend more time on their phones than those from families making $100,000 or more. Why? Screen media is cheaper than piano lessons. It is cheaper than after-school programs. Families who make less money have less money for extras.

How much time do you spend on the phone?

1. What percent of youth have smart phones by age 11?
   a.   95 percent.
   b.   53 percent.
   c.   7 percent.
   d.   30 percent.

2. What group spends an average of 7 hours per day on their phones?
   a.   tweens.
   b.   teens.
   c.   11-year-olds.
   d.   adults.

3. Who spends the most time on their phones?
   a.   youth taking piano lessons.
   b.   youth from families making over $100,000.
   c.   tweens.
   d.   youth from families making about $35,000 per year.

4. According to the article, multi-tasking was
   a.   counted once.
   b.   counted more than once.
   c.   was dangerous.
   d.   was done equally by teens and tweens.

Name: _____

The Cell Phone Revolution

A Pew Research study found that 53% of children in the U.S. get their first phone	16
by age 11. A study by "Common Sense Media" found that 95% of U.S. teens have their	33
own smart phone.	36
Seventy percent of those teens check social media several times per day. That is	50
up from 34% in 2012. And half of all teens say their phones distract them from their	67
homework. Their phones also distract them from the people they are with.	79
"Common Sense Media" also reported that teens spend 7 hours per day on their	93
phones. Tweens spend nearly 5 hours on theirs. But that doesn't mean real hours? The	108
study double counted multi-tasking, so what's the real number?	117
If a teen is texting a friend, streaming a video and is on social media for 10	134
minutes at one time – the study counted that as 30 minutes.	145
The study also pointed out that during those seven hours on their phones, teens	159
were also doing chores, riding on buses, in cars, socializing, eating meals – doing just	173
about everything else.	176
In sum, teens and their phones are joined. It is interesting to note that youth from	192
families making $35,000 per year spend more time on their phones than those from	206
families making $100,000 or more. Why? Screen media is cheaper than piano lessons.	219
It is cheaper than after-school programs. Families who make less money have less	233
money for extras.	236
How much time do you spend on the phone?	245

Words Read:	Words Read:	Words Read:
minus mistakes:	minus mistakes:	minus mistakes:
equals wpms:	equals wpms:	equals wpms:

Fantasy Football

Have you heard of Fantasy Football? Many teens have. According to PR Wire, almost 50% of teens play Fantasy Football.

For those who don't know, in fantasy football you are the owner or manager of a team. Your team plays other teams. Your team gets points based on real statistics.

Teams are in leagues. Points are scored on a weekly basis. The teams with the most points make it to fantasy post season.

The goal is to get the best players for your team. You form a team based on all of the NFL players. Each team has a quarterback, two running backs, and a flex player. Then you get two wide receivers and a tight end.

You also get to draft an entire NFL defense and special teams. Meaning that you don't pick individual players like you do for your offense. For example, you can have the entire Tampa Bay defense and special teams but not a mix from different teams.

You pick your teams in a draft. The draft works like the NFL draft does. Mostly.

Scoring rules vary from league to league. Make sure you know the scoring rules before you join a league. ESPN has a league. With ESPN, you get a Draft Kit to help you understand how Fantasy Football works.

Are you ready for some football?

1. If you play Fantasy Football, what is your role?
   a. player.
   b. quarterback.
   c. entire defense and offense.
   d. owner or manager.

2. According to the article, what percent of teens play Fantasy Football?
   a. about 30%.
   b. about 40%.
   c. about 50%.
   d. about 60%.

3. For your offense and special teams
   a. you choose individual players.
   b. you choose the offense of one NFL team for each.
   c. you choose the offense and special teams of one NFL team.
   d. the reading doesn't say.

4. Describe Fantasy Football.

_____

_____

_____

_____

_____

_____

Name: _____

Fantasy Football

Have you heard of Fantasy Football? Many teens have. According to PR Wire, 13
almost 50% of teens play Fantasy Football. 20

For those who don't know, in fantasy football you are the owner or manager of a 36
team. Your team plays other teams. Your team gets points based on real statistics. 50

Teams are in leagues. Points are scored on a weekly basis. The teams with the 65
most points make it to fantasy post season. 73

The goal is to get the best players for your team. You form a team based on all of 92
the NFL players. Each team has a quarterback, two running backs, and a flex player. 107
Then you get two wide receivers and a tight end. 117

You also get to draft an entire NFL defense and special teams. Meaning that you 132
don't pick individual players like you do for your offense. For example, you can have 147
the entire Tampa Bay defense and special teams but not a mix from different teams. 162

You pick your teams in a draft. The draft works like the NFL draft does. Mostly. 178

Scoring rules vary from league to league. Make sure you know the scoring rules 192
before you join a league. ESPN has a league. With ESPN, you get a Draft Kit to help 210
you understand how Fantasy Football works. 216

Are you ready for some football? 220

Words Read:	Words Read:	Words Read:
minus mistakes:	minus mistakes:	minus mistakes:
equals wpms:	equals wpms:	equals wpms:

Not Your Parent's Video Games

Teens today are the first group of people with grandparents who regularly played video games. The games of old, however, are nothing like video games today.

Video games came out in 1958. By the 1980s, games like PacMan and Space Invaders were in homes across the U.S. Today, games are more complex. They have more details.

Modern video games allow players to be part of the game. Players are like actors in movies. They watch themselves walk through what's on the screen.

Top games listed by teens include *Call of Duty* and *League of Legends.* *NBA2K20* is also popular. In these games, players are in the game. They play a role in what happens.

Games are often part of a series. The same games expand through time. This keeps games popular. Why? Because players can shape their characters. They can become their characters.

Here are some interesting facts about video games. Over 75% of people in the US have at least one gamer in their household. Gamers are more likely to play an instrument than non-gamers. Males are more likely than females to play video games but only 8% more likely.

When was the last time you played a video game? What is your favorite?

1. Video games came out in
    a. 1980.
    b. the 1980s.
    c. 1958.
    d. 1970.

2. Today, top games include
    a. PacMan and Space Invaders.
    b. Call of Duty and PacMan.
    c. League of Legends and PacMan.
    d. Call of Duty and League of Legends.

3. How are series special?
    a. they add to the game.
    b. they turn games into movies.
    c. they allow players to develop their characters.
    d. they have toys that come with games.

4. According to the article, how many people in the U.S. have at least one gamer in the household?
    a. 8%.
    b. 94%.
    c. 75%.
    d. 58%.

Not Your Parent's Video Games

Teens today are the first group of people with grandparents who regularly played	13
video games. The games of old, however, are nothing like video games today.	26
Video games came out in 1958. By the 1980s, games like PacMan and Space	40
Invaders were in homes across the U.S. Today, games are more complex. They have	54
more details.	56
Modern video games allow players to be part of the game. Players are like actors	71
in movies. They watch themselves walk through what's on the screen.	82
Top games listed by teens include *Call of Duty* and *League of Legends. NBA2K20*	96
is also popular. In these games, players are in the game. They play a role in what	113
happens.	114
Games are often part of a series. The same games expand through time. This	128
keeps games popular. Why? Because players can shape their characters. They can	140
become their characters.	143
Here are some interesting facts about video games. Over 75% of people in the US	158
have at least one gamer in their household. Gamers are more likely to play an	173
instrument than non-gamers. Males are more likely than females to play video games	187
but only 8% more likely.	192
When was the last time you played a video game? What is your favorite?	206

Words Read:	Words Read:	Words Read:
minus mistakes:	minus mistakes:	minus mistakes:
equals wpms:	equals wpms:	equals wpms:

Things to Learn

1. **Foreign Language:** A new language helps with school, jobs and travel.

2. **Learn an Instrument:** No one is cooler than a musical artist! Creating music brings joy to both the player and the listener.

3. **Learn to Sew:** Make a mask. Sew a shirt. Make a quilt. Following a pattern and making something from nothing can be super rewarding.

4. **Learn to Sign:** You can learn from a book, online or in person. Signing can even lead to a job as an interpreter.

5. **Make Greeting Cards:** Do you have an artistic flair? Make a greeting card or two. Have a real talent? Take them to a local retailer and make a little money.

6. **Camp in Your Back Yard:** Invite over some friends and have a camp out. Make s'mores, look up at the stars and tell ghost stories.

7. **Have a Garage Sale:** Gather things you don't want and sell them. Donate the money to someone in need.

8. **Buy Something Repurposed:** Buy something second hand. People sell lots of things that are still good. Bonus, it is good for the planet.

9. **Buy Something You Wouldn't Wear:** Go extreme or traditional. Make it something that isn't you. Mix it up. Have fun.

---

1. What item in the reading do you need an "artistic flair" for?
   - a.   painting.
   - b.   sign language.
   - c.   learning to fly.
   - d.   making a greeting card.

2. What item does the article suggest you to "mix it up?"
   - a.   Have a Garage Sale.
   - b.   Learn to Sew.
   - c.   Learn to Sign.
   - d.   Buy Something You Wouldn't Wear.

3. Which item number would you do in the dark?
   - a.   Camp in Your Backyard.
   - b.   Have a Garage Sale.
   - c.   Learn a Foreign Language.
   - d.   Learn to Sew.

4. If you "make a mask" you will need to
   - a.   Camp in Your Backyard.
   - b.   Have a Garage Sale.
   - c.   Learn a Foreign Language.
   - d.   Learn to Sew.

5. Turn the article into a paragraph.

_____

_____

_____

_____

_____

Name: _____

Things to Learn

1. **Foreign Language:** A new language helps with school, jobs and travel. | 11
2. **Learn an Instrument:** No one is cooler than a musical artist! Creating music brings | 25
   joy to both the player and the listener. | 33
3. **Learn to Sew:** Make a mask. Sew a shirt. Make a quilt. Following a pattern and | 49
   making something from nothing can be super rewarding. | 57
4. **Learn to Sign:** You can learn from a book, online or in person. Signing can even | 73
   lead to a job as an interpreter. | 80
5. **Make Greeting Cards:** Do you have an artistic flair? Make a greeting card or two. | 95
   Have a real talent? Take them to a local retailer and make a little money. | 110
6. **Camp in Your Back Yard:** Invite over some friends and have a camp out. Make | 125
   s'mores, look up at the stars and tell ghost stories. | 135
7. **Have a Garage Sale:** Gather things you don't want and sell them. Donate the | 149
   money to someone in need. | 154
8. **Buy Something Repurposed:** Buy something second hand. People sell lots of things | 166
   that are still good. Bonus, it is good for the planet. | 177
9. **Buy Something You Wouldn't Wear:** Go extreme or traditional. Make it something | 189
   that isn't you. Mix it up. Have fun. | 197

Words Read:	Words Read:	Words Read:
minus mistakes:	minus mistakes:	minus mistakes:
equals wpms:	equals wpms:	equals wpms:

Name: _____

National "Go Skateboarding Day"

June 21 is **Go Skateboarding Day**. It began in 2004. The idea of **Go Skateboarding Day** is to get skateboarding out to more people.

By 2006, the small event was in more than 32 countries. Today, on June 21, skaters pair with sponsors and parks to host events.

Skaters gather together and twist and turn through the air. They show their talent. They have tons of fun.

How can you celebrate **Go Skateboarding Day**? Get the word out on social media with #GoSkateboardingDay. Ask your neighborhood, city, or town to host an event. Show off your skills. If you skate, help people who can't.

You can also make a skateboarding video. Be sure to post it. Your video can be awesome. It can be funny. It can be anything you want.

A great way to celebrate the day is to learn a new trick. How about the **Kick Flip Trick**? If you are new to the sport, this trick is for you. In this trick, you lift the wheels of the board and twirl it under you.

The **Heal Flip Trick** is also a good one. In this trick, you lift the nose of the board. Use your back foot for the lift and then jump. When you are in the air, put your finger on the nose of your board and flick it up. Land your feet back on the board.

If you celebrate the day, don't forget your knee and elbow pads. It is **Go Skateboarding Day**, not "Go to the Hospital Day."

1. Go Skateboarding Day started to
   a. raise awareness for skating.
   b. raise money for skating.
   c. get skateboarding out to more people.
   d. teach more people how to skate.

2. Go Skateboarding Day began in
   a. 2004.
   b. 2006.
   c. 1970.
   d. 1958.

3. Which of the following is **not** listed as a way to celebrate the day?
   a. Go to skateboard camp.
   b. Learn a new trick.
   c. Teach someone to skate.
   d. Ask to host an event.

4. Tricks to learn for the day include
   a. Kick Flip Trick.
   b. Flip Kick Trick.
   c. Heal Kick Trick.
   d. Kick Heal Trick.

5. Summarize the passage.

_____

_____

_____

_____

_____

National "Go Skateboarding Day"

June 21 is Go Skateboarding Day. It began in 2004. The idea of Go Skateboarding	15
Day is to get skateboarding out to more people.	23
By 2006, the small event was in more than 32 countries. Today, on June 21,	38
skaters pair with sponsors and parks to host events.	47
Skaters gather together and twist and turn through the air. They show their talent.	61
They have tons of fun.	66
How can you celebrate Go Skateboarding Day? Get the word out on social media	80
with #GoSkateboardingDay. Ask your neighborhood, city, or town to host an event.	92
Show off your skills. If you skate, help people who can't.	103
You can also make a skateboarding video. Be sure to post it. Your video can be	119
awesome. It can be funny. It can be anything you want.	130
A great way to celebrate the day is to learn a new trick. How about the Kick Flip	148
Trick? If you are new to the sport, this trick is for you. In this trick, you lift the wheels	158
of the board and twirl it under you.	166
The Heal Flip Trick is also a good one. In this trick, you lift the nose of the board.	185
Use your back foot for the lift and then jump. When you are in the air, put your finger	204
on the nose of your board and flick it up. Land your feet back on the board.	221
If you celebrate the day, don't forget your knee and elbow pads. It is Go	236
Skateboarding Day, not "Go to the Hospital Day."	244

Words Read:	Words Read:	Words Read:
minus mistakes:	minus mistakes:	minus mistakes:
equals wpms:	equals wpms:	equals wpms:

Name: _____

Skateboarding Heroes

There are many great skateboarders in the world. Here are a few of the best.

Danny Way is from California. He's won *Thrasher* magazine's "Skater of the Year" two times. He is known for his extreme tricks. He once jumped onto a skateboard ramp from a helicopter.

Eric Koston began skating at age 11. By 17, he was already a pro. He's won many titles. He's also been in Tony Hawk's video games *Skate2* and *Skate3*.

Lizzie Armanto grew up in Santa Monica, California. Her mom is American. Her dad is from Finland. She credits her success to her mom. She is the first woman to complete Tony Hawk's 360-loop ramp. Lizzie has also represented the U.S. in the Summer X Games.

Last, but not least, is Tony Hawk. Tony Hawk is one of the best-known skateboarders in the world. Tony an award-winning skateboarder. He is also a video game developer, activist, and more.

Tony Hawk is skateboarding. Born in San Diego, California, Tony helped define the sport. Tony did not do well in school. Then they found he was gifted. Smart beyond smart, he was put in harder classes and did well. He became a pro-skateboarder at age fourteen. He's won the World Skateboard Championship twelve years in a row.

There are many great skateboarders. Do you know any not listed here?

1. Which of the following is not mentioned as a skateboard hero?
   a.   Tony Hawk
   b.   Danny Way
   c.   Danny Armanto
   d.   Lizzie Armanto

2. Which skateboarder mentioned has a mom from Finland and a dad from America?
   a.   Lizzie Armento.
   b.   Eric Koston.
   c.   Tony Hawk.
   d.   no one mentioned.

3. According to the passage, one of the best-known skateboarders in the world is
   a.   Tony Hawk
   b.   Danny Way
   c.   Eric Koston
   d.   Lizzie Armanto

4. Which skateboarder in the passage turned pro at fourteen?
   a.   Tony Hawk
   b.   Danny Way
   c.   Danny Armanto
   d.   Lizzie Armanto

5. Write two things in the article that you want to know more about.

_____

_____

_____

_____

_____

Name: _____

Skateboarding Heroes

There are many great skateboarders in the world. Here are a few of the best.	15
Danny Way is from California. He's won *Thrasher* magazine's "Skater of the Year"	28
two times. He is known for his extreme tricks. He once jumped onto a skateboard ramp	44
from a helicopter.	47
Eric Koston began skating at age 11. By 17, he was already a pro. He's won many	64
titles. He's also been in Tony Hawk's video games *Skate2* and *Skate3*.	76
Lizzie Armanto grew up in Santa Monica, California. Her mom is American. Her	89
dad is from Finland. She credits her success to her mom. She is the first woman to	106
complete Tony Hawk's 360-loop ramp. Lizzie has also represented the U.S. in the	120
Summer X Games.	123
Last, but not least, is Tony Hawk. Tony Hawk is one of the best-known	138
skateboarders in the world. Tony an award-winning skateboarder. He is also a video	152
game developer, activist, and more.	157
Tony Hawk is skateboarding. Born in San Diego, California, Tony helped define the	170
sport. Tony did not do well in school. Then they found he was gifted. Smart beyond	186
smart, he was put in harder classes and did well. He became a pro-skateboarder at	202
age fourteen. He's won the World Skateboard Championship twelve years in a row.	215
There are many great skateboarders. Do you know any not listed here?	227

Words Read:	Words Read:	Words Read:
minus mistakes:	minus mistakes:	minus mistakes:
equals wpms:	equals wpms:	equals wpms:

Name: _____

National Pizza Day

Cheese or pepperoni? Thin crust or deep dish? Whatever you like – pizza is one of America's favorite foods.

February 9th is National Pizza Day, so grab slice. It is a day to eat as much pizza as you want.

Pizza is from Italy. In 10th century Italy there are records of a cheesy flat bread with sauce. In America, pizza made its mark in 1905. The first National Pizza day was in 2000. Who started it? No one knows. No one knows, but it is a day to get great deals on pizza all over the U.S.

Here are some interesting facts about pizza:

- Over 3 billion pizzas are sold in the U.S. each year. Four billion if you count frozen pizzas.
- About 350 slices of pizza are eaten per second.
- Pepperoni is the most popular topping.
- 17% of U.S. restaurants are pizzerias.
- The first pizzeria was opened in 1738 in Italy.
- The first U.S. pizzeria was opened in 1895.
- The first US pizzeria was opened in New York City.
- 94% of Americans eat pizza often.
- 93% of Americans have eaten pizza in the last month.

What is your favorite kind of pizza?

1. According to the article, America's favorite pizza is
    a. cheese.
    b. sausage.
    c. veggie.
    d. pepperoni.

2. The first pizza dates back to
    a. 2000.
    b. 1905.
    c. 10th Century Italy.
    d. 10th Century U.S.

3. In the U.S., about
    a. 3 million slices are eaten per day
    b. 3 billion slices are eaten per day
    c. 350 slices per second
    d. 3 million slices per second

4. The first US pizzeria was opened in
    a. 1738.
    b. 2000.
    c. 1895.
    d. 1905.

5. Summarize the article in **two** sentences.

_____

_____

_____

_____

_____

_____

Name: _____

National Pizza Day

    Cheese or pepperoni? Thin crust or deep dish? Whatever you like – pizza is one of   15

America's favorite foods.   18

    February 9th is National Pizza Day, so grab slice. It is a day to eat as much pizza   36

as you want.   39

    Pizza is from Italy. In 10th century Italy there are records of a cheesy flat bread   55

with sauce. In America, pizza made its mark in 1905. The first National Pizza day was   71

in 2000. Who started it? No one knows. No one knows, but it is a day to get great deals   91

on pizza all over the U.S.   97

    Here are some interesting facts about pizza: 104

- Over 3 billion pizzas are sold in the U.S. each year. Four billion if you count   120
  frozen pizzas.   122
- About 350 slices of pizza are eaten per second.   131
- Pepperoni is the most popular topping.   137
- 17% of U.S. restaurants are pizzerias.   143
- The first pizzeria was opened in 1738 in Italy.   152
- The first U.S. pizzeria was opened in 1895.   160
- The first US pizzeria was opened in New York City.   170
- 94% of Americans eat pizza often.   176
- 93% of Americans have eaten pizza in the last month.   186

What is your favorite kind of pizza?   193

Words Read:	Words Read:	Words Read:
minus mistakes:	minus mistakes:	minus mistakes:
equals wpms:	equals wpms:	equals wpms:

Major key				
I	V	V		I
i	III	III		i
Minor key	(or V)	(or V)		

Music

Music makes us feel good. It changes our moods. It helps us relax. It pumps us up. It brings us together. Music is a part of our lives in many ways.

Most teens love music. A lot. In fact, teens spend more time listening to music than hanging out with their friends. According to *Rolling Stone* magazine, the five top types of music are rock, dance, pop, hip hop, and rap.

Rock started in the U.S. in the 1950s. At the time, rock and roll music was a sign of risk. It was a sign of rebelling against adults. In the U.S., 28% of teens favor rock music.

During the 80s club culture raged. With it came dance music. DJs mixed tracks and teens gathered to enjoy. Dance music has a strong beat. It has electronic tones. It is still popular today.

Pop is the most popular music with teens. Over 52% of teens listen to pop. Pop music has simple tunes. It is catchy. Lyrics repeat. Pop songs are easy to sing. Pop can include country music.

Hip Hop began in the 1970s. The digital remix exists because of hip hop. Hip hop is rooted in struggle. It is easier to master than other types of music.

Rap rounds out the list. Rap music is heavy in vocals. The vocals are done over a beat. Rap is related to hip hop. Lyrics are risky. Rap is to teens what rock was in the 50s.

Whether it is rock or pop – hip hip or rap – we love our music. That is not going to change anytime soon.

1. According to the article, the top five types of music are
   a. rock, dance, pop, hip hop, and rap.
   b. rock, country, pop, hip hop, and rap.
   c. rock, pop, hip hop, teen, and rap.
   d. rock, dance, pop, country, and rap.

2. Pop music is favored by _____ percent of teens
   a. 28%.
   b. 80 %.
   c. 52 %.
   d. 50%.

3. According to the article, hip hop music began in the
   a. 1950s.
   b. 1970s.
   c. 1980s.
   d. 1990s.

4. According to the article, _____ is heavy in vocals
   a. rock.
   b. pop.
   c. dance.
   d. rap.

5. Summarize the article in **two** sentences.

_____

_____

_____

_____

Name: _____

Music

Music makes us feel good. It changes our moods. It helps us relax. It pumps us up. | 17

It brings us together. Music is a part of our lives in many ways. | 31

Most teens love music. A lot. In fact, teens spend more time listening to music than | 47

hanging out with their friends. According to *Rolling Stone* magazine, the five top types | 61

of music are rock, dance, pop, hip hop, and rap. | 71

Rock started in the U.S. in the 1950s. At the time, rock and roll music was a sign of | 90

risk. It was a sign of rebelling against adults. In the U.S., 28% of teens favor rock | 107

music. | 108

During the 80s club culture raged. With it came dance music. DJs mixed tracks | 122

and teens gathered to enjoy. Dance music has a strong beat. It has electronic tones. It | 138

is still popular today. | 142

Pop is the most popular music with teens. Over 52% of teens listen to pop. Pop | 158

music has simple tunes. It is catchy. Lyrics repeat. Pop songs are easy to sing. Pop | 174

can include country music. | 178

Hip Hop began in the 1970s. The digital remix exists because of hip hop. Hip hop is | 195

rooted in struggle. It is easier to master than other types of music. | 208

Rap rounds out the list. Rap music is heavy in vocals. The vocals are done over a | 225

beat. Rap is related to hip hop. Lyrics are risky. Rap is to teens what rock was in the | 244

50s. | 245

Whether it is rock or pop – hip hip or rap – we love our music. That is not going to | 264

change anytime soon. | 267

Words Read:	Words Read:	Words Read:
minus mistakes:	minus mistakes:	minus mistakes:
equals wpms:	equals wpms:	equals wpms:

Name: _____

Rapper Young Thug

Young Thug was born in Atlanta. His real name is Jeffery Williams. He is 29-years-old. He was one of the most popular rappers of 2020.

Young Thug came to fame 2014. He began his career on rapper TruRoyals' song *She Can Go*.

Young Thug raps alone and on tracks with other rappers. He's also been on tracks with pop stars. His first solo album was in 2019. It was called *So Much Fun*. The album hit number one on the U.S. *Billboard 200* list.

Songs from the album reached 11 and 12 on the same list. *The London* hit 11 and *Hot* hit 12. In 2020, the title *Go Crazy* reached number 9.

Young Thug is one of 11 children. He grew up in the projects of Atlanta. A project is part of public housing.

In 2014, he recorded songs with Kanye West. In June of the same year, Young Thug signed with the label 300 Entertainment.

In 2015, a data breach leaked 100s of Young Thugs tracks to the internet. There were rumors about who managed him. There were rumors about who would release his next album. Young Thug set the record straight. "I manage myself. I have a deal with Atlantic." He released several tracks early. He feared another leak.

Young Thug is known for his special voice. *Pitchfork* said he has a "weird approach to rapping...that works." Young Thug mixes rap with pop. He uses both to hook his listeners.

Young Thug has six children. He is engaged. He lives in Buckhead, Atlanta.

Photo by **Frank Schwichtenberg** Creative Commons License.

1. Young Thug lives in
   a.   Atlanta.
   b.   Buckhead, Atlanta.
   c.   Los Angeles.
   d.   New York.

2. Young Thug's first solo album was
   a.   London.
   b.   She Can Go.
   c.   So Much Fun.
   d.   an album with Kanye West.

3. According to his article, the title *Go Crazy* reached _____ on the charts
   a.   11.
   b.   12.
   c.   9.
   d.   20.

4. According to the article, who manages Young Thug?
   a.   Atlanta.
   b.   Kanye West.
   c.   Entertainment.
   d.   himself.

5. Summarize the article in **one** sentence.

_____

_____

_____

Rapper Young Thug

Young Thug was born in Atlanta. His real name is Jeffery Williams. He is 29-years-	16
old. He was one of the most popular rappers of 2020.	27
Young Thug came to fame 2014. He began his career on rapper TruRoyals' song	41
She Can Go.	44
Young Thug raps alone and on tracks with other rappers. He's also been on tracks	59
with pop stars. His first solo album was in 2019. It was called *So Much Fun.* The album	77
hit number one on the U.S. *Billboard 200* list.	86
Songs from the album reached 11 and 12 on the same list. *The London* hit 11 and	103
Hot hit 12. In 2020, the title *Go Crazy* reached number 9.	115
Young Thug is one of 11 children. He grew up in the projects of Atlanta. A project is	133
part of public housing.	137
In 2014, he recorded songs with Kanye West. In June of the same year, Young	152
Thug signed with the label 300 Entertainment.	159
In 2015, a data breach leaked 100s of Young Thugs tracks to the internet. There	174
were rumors about who managed him. There were rumors about who would release	187
his next album. Young Thug set the record straight. "I manage myself. I have a deal	203
with Atlantic." He released several tracks early. He feared another leak.	214
Young Thug is known for his special voice. *Pitchfork* said he has a "weird approach	229
to rapping…that works." Young Thug mixes rap with pop. He uses both to hook his	244
listeners.	245
Young Thug has six children. He is engaged. He lives in Buckhead, Atlanta.	258

Words Read:	Words Read:	Words Read:
minus mistakes:	minus mistakes:	minus mistakes:
equals wpms:	equals wpms:	equals wpms:

Name: _____

Kanye West

Kanye West is a rapper. He is a record producer. He is a fashion designer. He is an influencer. Kanye West is a force in the entertainment world.

Kanye was born in Atlanta. He moved to Chicago when he was a boy. His birthday is June 8, 1977.

When Kanye was 10, he moved to China with his mom. She was a university professor. He was the only person in his class who wasn't Chinese. He didn't care. He fit in well. He learned the language quickly. He did well in school. He did well in school in China and in the United States.

Kanye began writing poetry when he was five. He started rapping in the third grade. He also recorded his first track in the third grade.

He went to Chicago State University. Classes got in the way of his music. He dropped out. His mother was not happy. That changed when his music career took off.

Kanye is one of the world's best-selling musical artists. He's sold over 20 million albums worldwide. He has also sold over 140 million singles. He's won 21 Grammy Awards. He's won many other awards. Six of his albums were included on *Rolling Stone's* 2020 *500 Greatest Albums of All Time.*

Kanye West was married to Kim Kardashian. They have four children. He lives in Wyoming.

1. Kanya West moved to China when he was

    a.   in the third grade.

    b.   10.

    c.   in college.

    d.   in high school.

2. Kanye West recorded his first song when he was

    a.   in the third grade.

    b.   when he was 10.

    c.   in college.

    d.   in high school.

3. According to his article, Kanye has sold over

    a.   140 million singles.

    b.   140 million albums.

    c.   20 million singles.

    d.   20 million tracks.

4. According to the article, how did Kanye do in school?

    a.   well.

    b.   poorly.

    c.   it doesn't say.

    d.   he was a fair student.

5. Summarize the article in **one** sentence.

_____

_____

Kanye West

Kanye West is a rapper. He is a record producer. He is a fashion designer. He is an	18
influencer. Kanye West is a force in the entertainment world.	28

Kanye was born in Atlanta. He moved to Chicago when he was a boy. His birthday   44
is June 8, 1977.   48

When Kanye was 10, he moved to China with his mom. She was a university   63
professor. He was the only person in his class who wasn't Chinese. He didn't care. He   79
fit in well. He learned the language quickly. He did well in school. He did well in school   97
in China and in the United States.   104

Kanye began writing poetry when he was five. He started rapping in the third   118
grade. He also recorded his first track in the third grade.   129

He went to Chicago State University. Classes got in the way of his music. He   144
dropped out. His mother was not happy. That changed when his music career took off.   159

Kanye is one of the world's best-selling musical artists. He's sold over 20 million   174
albums worldwide. He has also sold over 140 million singles. He's won 21 Grammy   188
Awards. He's won many other awards. Six of his albums were included on *Rolling*   202
Stone's 2020 *500 Greatest Albums of All Time.*   210

Kanye West was married to Kim Kardashian. They have four children. He lives in   224
Wyoming.   225

Words Read:	Words Read:	Words Read:
minus mistakes:	minus mistakes:	minus mistakes:
equals wpms:	equals wpms:	equals wpms:

Name: _____

Cardi B

Cardi B was born in New York City on October 11, 1992. Cardi B is a U.S. rapper and songwriter.

Cardi B started on the internet. She became popular on Vine and Instagram. From 2015 to 2016, she was a cast member on VH1's show *Love & Hip Hop*.

Cardi B's first studio album was in 2018. It was called *Invasion of Privacy*. The album went triple platinum. Triple platinum means over 3 million copies were sold. She was the first female rap artist to be nominated for the *Album of the Year* Grammy.

Cardi B is a trend-setter. About fashion, she's said she doesn't care how much something costs. "I don't care if it costs $2000 or $15. If it looks good on me, it looks good on me."

Cardi B lives in New Jersey. She works out of New York City. She lives in New Jersey because it is cheaper than living in NYC.

Cardi B uses her fame to help other female rappers and hip-hop artists. *The New Yorker* gives her credit for opening the door for women. She gives hope to have-nots.

Cardi B is married to rapper Offset. They have an on again, off again, marriage. They have one daughter.

You can follow both Cardi B and Offset on Instagram.

1. According to the article, Cardi B is all of the following except
    a.   a rapper.
    b.   a songwriter.
    c.   a hip-hop artist.
    d.   a fashion designer.

2. Cardi B was the first female rapper to be nominated for
    a.   a Grammy
    b.   Album of the Year Grammy
    c.   the New Yorker award
    d.   Artist of the Year Grammy

3. According to his article, Cardi B uses her fame to
    a.   sell shoes.
    b.   help other rappers.
    c.   help other female rappers.
    d.   help her daughter.

4. According to the article, where does Cardi B live?
    a.   New York.
    b.   New Jersey.
    c.   Vine.
    d.   the article doesn't say.

5. Summarize the article in **one** sentence.

_____

_____

_____

_____

_____

Cardi B

Cardi B was born in New York City on October 11, 1992. Cardi B is a U.S. rapper and songwriter. | 19
20

Cardi B started on the internet. She became popular on Vine and Instagram. From 2015 to 2016, she was a cast member on VH1's show *Love & Hip Hop*. | 34
49

Cardi B's first studio album was in 2018. It was called *Invasion of Privacy*. The album went triple platinum. Triple platinum means over 3 million copies were sold. She was the first female rap artist to be nominated for the *Album of the Year* Grammy. | 64
78
94

Cardi B is a trend-setter. About fashion, she's said she doesn't care how much something costs. "I don't care if it costs $2000 or $15. If it looks good on me, it looks good on me." | 109
128
131

Cardi B lives in New Jersey. She works out of New York City. She lives in New Jersey because it is cheaper than living in NYC. | 148
157

Cardi B uses her fame to help other female rappers and hip-hop artists. *The New Yorker* gives her credit for opening the door for women. She gives hope to have-nots. | 173
189

Cardi B is married to rapper Offset. They have an on again, off again, marriage. They have one daughter. | 204
208

You can follow both Cardi B and Offset on Instagram. | 218

Words Read:	Words Read:	Words Read:
minus mistakes:	minus mistakes:	minus mistakes:
equals wpms:	equals wpms:	equals wpms:

Emma Watson

Emma Watson was born on April 15, 1990. She was born in Paris. She was raised in England. She rose to fame in the Harry Potter movies as Hermione Granger.

Watson went on to star as Belle the remake of Disney's *Beauty and the Beast*. She went to Brown University. She earned a degree in English literature.

Watson is also a model. She's worked for many brands. One is People Tree. People Tree makes clothes that do not hurt the environment. Watson was the youngest person ever to be on the cover of Teen Vogue.

Watson works for the education of girls. She believes that girls can do anything.

Emma Watson Fun Facts:

- She has two cats. They are named Bubbles and Domino.
- Her favorite Harry Potter book is <u>Harry Potter and the Prisoner of Azkaban.</u>
- She was named after her grandmother. The one on her father's side.
- She and her Harry Potter co-stars were named #9 on Entertainment Weekly's Best Entertainers of the Year in 2005.
- By 2009, her film work had made over 5.4 billion dollars.

What is your favorite Emma Watson film?

1. Emma Watson rose to fame in what films?
   a. Disney
   b. Beauty and the Beast Series
   c. Harry Potter Series
   d. People Tree

2. Emma earned a degree from Brown University in
   a. British literature.
   b. English literature.
   c. acting.
   d. literature.

3. Emma Watson's pets are named
   a. Baubles and Bubbles.
   b. Bubbles and Domino.
   c. Baubles and Domino.
   d. Domino and Harry.

4. Who is Emma Watson named after?
   a. her grandmother on her mom's side.
   b. her father's mother.
   c. her father's grandmother.
   d. her mother's grandmother.

5. Summarize the article in **one** sentence

_____

_____

_____

_____

_____

_____

Name: _____

Emma Watson

Emma Watson was born on April 15, 1990. She was born in Paris. She was raised in England. She rose to fame in the Harry Potter movies as Hermione Granger.

Watson went on to star as Belle the remake of Disney's *Beauty and the Beast*. She went to Brown University. She earned a degree in English literature.

Watson is also a model. She's worked for many brands. One is People Tree. People Tree makes clothes that do not hurt the environment. Watson was the youngest person ever to be on the cover of Teen Vogue.

Watson works for the education of girls. She believes that girls can do anything.

Emma Watson Fun Facts:

- She has two cats. They are named Bubbles and Domino.
- Her favorite Harry Potter book is <u>Harry Potter and the Prisoner of Azkaban.</u>
- She was named after her grandmother. The one on her father's side.
- She and her Harry Potter co-stars were named #9 on Entertainment Weekly's Best Entertainers of the Year in 2005.
- By 2009, her film work had made over 5.4 billion dollars.

What is your favorite Emma Watson film?

Line	Count
Emma Watson was born on April 15, 1990. She was born in Paris. She was raised in	17
England. She rose to fame in the Harry Potter movies as Hermione Granger.	30
Watson went on to star as Belle the remake of Disney's *Beauty and the Beast*. She	46
went to Brown University. She earned a degree in English literature.	47
Watson is also a model. She's worked for many brands. One is People Tree. People	62
Tree makes clothes that do not hurt the environment. Watson was the youngest	75
person ever to be on the cover of Teen Vogue.	85
Watson works for the education of girls. She believes that girls can do anything.	99
Emma Watson Fun Facts:	103
She has two cats. They are named Bubbles and Domino.	113
Her favorite Harry Potter book is Harry Potter and the Prisoner of Azkaban.	126
She was named after her grandmother. The one on her father's side.	138
She and her Harry Potter co-stars were named #9 on Entertainment Weekly's Best	152
Entertainers of the Year in 2005.	158
By 2009, her film work had made over 5.4 billion dollars.	169
What is your favorite Emma Watson film?	176

Words Read:	Words Read:	Words Read:
minus mistakes:	minus mistakes:	minus mistakes:
equals wpms:	equals wpms:	equals wpms:

Name: _____

The Notch

Born: June 1, 1979
Birthplace: Stockholm Sweden
Occupation: Actress, activist, director, producer
Known For: Creating Minecraft

People call him Notch. He is a game developer. His most successful game to date was developed in 2009. It was called "Cave Game." It was for PCs. The only people who played "Cave Game" where those who liked to code and design gaming worlds. But you know the game. "Cave Game" is the beta version of Minecraft.

This first (beta) version of Minecraft was basic. It was also more than just a game for building. It allowed players to gather the resources they needed to build. And there's more. Players could create more than just structures. They could create tools they needed. They could fight monsters. They could explore a large world. That world kept getting bigger and bigger and bigger.

Minecraft has always had a simple look. Very basic shapes that look like pixels. The low-end graphics are helpful. They allow people to build almost anything. They also work faster. No detailed graphics – no high-speed processing needed.

A full version of the game was not released until 2011. Millions of copies were sold. And an industry was born.

1. What video game did Notch create?
   a. Call of Duty
   b. Minecraft
   c. Pac Man
   d. Minecreator

2. The game's low-end graphics make it
   a. easier to play.
   b. faster due to low end graphics
   c. faster due to more pixels.
   d. faster because there is no high-speed processing necessary.

3. The earliest version of the game
   a. was called Cave Mine.
   b. was for building.
   c. was for more than just building.
   d. ran faster because of limited graphics.

4. The original game was
   a. only for PlayStation.
   b. only for fighting monsters.
   c. only for PC.
   d. was developed for builders exclusively.

5. Write the main idea of the reading in complete sentences.

_____

_____

_____

_____

_____

_____

_____

The Notch

People call him Notch. He is a game developer. His most successful game to date	15
was developed in 2009. It was called "Cave Game." It was for PCs. The only people	31
who played "Cave Game" where those who liked to code and design gaming worlds.	45
But you know the game. "Cave Game" is the beta version of Minecraft.	58
This first (beta) version of Minecraft was basic. It was also more than just a game	74
for building. It allowed players to gather the resources they needed to build. And	88
there's more. Players could create more than just structures. They could create tools	101
they needed. They could fight monsters. They could explore a large world. That world	115
kept getting bigger and bigger and bigger.	122
Minecraft has always had a simple look. Very basic shapes that look like pixels. The	137
low-end graphics are helpful. They allow people to build almost anything. They also	151
work faster. No detailed graphics – no high-speed processing needed.	161
A full version of the game was not released until 2011. Millions of copies were sold.	177
And an industry was born.	182

Words Read:	Words Read:	Words Read:
minus mistakes:	minus mistakes:	minus mistakes:
equals wpms:	equals wpms:	equals wpms:

Name: _____

Sheila Johnson

Born: January 25, 1949
Birthplace: McKeesport, Pennsylvania
High School: Proviso East High School
College: University of Illinois
Degree: Bachelor's of Arts, Music
After College: Worked as a music teacher
Awards: 2007 Virginia Women in History
Best Known For: Giving away a lot of money

Sheila Johnson isn't a household name. She should be. She is one of America's most successful self-made woman. What is Sheila's claim to fame? Sheila Johnson co-founded B.E.T. – Black Entertainment Network.

Black Entertainment Network was founded in 1979. Sheila started the network with her then-husband. Viacom bought B.E.T. from the couple in 2001. In 2002, Sheila divorced her husband. She sold off her shares of B.E.T. She started investing in hotels in Virginia. She started investing in hotels in Florida. She also invested in other real estate and in horses.

Sheila produces movies, too. In 2013, she produced **The Butler. The Butler** is the story of a former slave who went on to work for the White House. Sheila is also the only black woman to own pieces of three pro-sports teams. Sheila owns part of the WNBA Mystics. She also owns pieces of the NBA Wizards and NHL Capitals.

Sheila is the first African-American woman to have a net worth of one billion dollars. She believes in helping others. She's founded numerous charities and has given millions to schools – from the middle school where her son went to colleges all over the country. Sheila Johnson is one of America's successful women, and she certainly pays that forward.

1. Right after college, Sheila Johnson worked as a
   a. college professor.
   b. film producer.
   c. music teacher.
   d. television network administrator.

2. Sheila and her husband founded B.E.T in
   a. 1949.
   b. 1979.
   c. 2002.
   d. 2001.

3. Sheila was the first
   a. African American woman to make1 billion dollars.
   b. African American woman to produce movies.
   c. co-founder of B.E.T.
   d. woman to win the **2007 Virginia Women in History** award.

4. Sheila sold her shares in B.E.T. and purchased
   a. rights to produce the film **The Butler.**
   b. real estate and horses.
   c. hotels and cars.
   d. sports teams and television network.

5. Write the main idea of the reading in complete sentences.

   _____

   _____

   _____

   _____

   _____

Shelia Johnson

Sheila Johnson isn't a household name. She should be. She is one of America's most	15
successful self-made woman. What is Sheila's claim to fame? Sheila Johnson co-	28
founded B.E.T. – Black Entertainment Network.	33
Black Entertainment Network was founded in 1979. Sheila started the network with	45
her then-husband. Viacom bought B.E.T. from the couple in 2001. In 2002, Sheila	59
divorced her husband. She sold off her shares of B.E.T. She started investing in hotels	74
in Virginia. She started investing in hotels in Florida. She also invested in other real	89
estate and in horses.	93
Sheila produces movies, too. In 2013, she produced *The Butler*. *The Butler* is the	107
story of a former slave who went on to work for the White House. Sheila is also the	125
only black woman to own pieces of three pro-sports teams. Sheila owns part of the	141
WNBA Mystics. She also owns pieces of the NBA Wizards and NHL Capitals.	154
Sheila is the first African-American woman to have a net worth of one billion	169
dollars. She believes in helping others. She's founded numerous charities and has	181
given millions to schools – from the middle school where her son went to colleges all	196
over the country. Sheila Johnson is one of America's successful women, and she	209
certainly pays that forward.	213

Words Read:	Words Read:	Words Read:
minus mistakes:	minus mistakes:	minus mistakes:
equals wpms:	equals wpms:	equals wpms:

Name: _____

Making a Lot of Money vs. Being Rich: Sophia Bush

Bush at the 6th Annual Hollywood Style Awards
CC BY-SA 3.0.

Born: July 8, 1982
Birthplace: Pasadena, California
Occupation: Actress, activist, director, producer
Activist: Raises awareness for cancer, going green and politics
College: University of Southern California
Degree: Bachelor's of Arts, Journalism
Entrepreneur: Detroit Blows.

Sophia Bush is a lot of things. Sophia Bush is an actress. Sophia Bush is an investor. Sophia Bush is also the co-founder of Detroit Blows. Detroit Blows is a beauty salon in Detroit that uses non-toxic products, but that is not the point. What is the point? You can make a lot of money working a job, but it is rare to become rich unless you own part or all of a business. That is a motto Sophia lives by.

"I have a positive relationship with money. I focus on what I have. On what I can do. It is too easy to fear money. I think that having a positive relationship is necessary. I think working hard is necessary. Put those two together and you can do anything."

Sophia, started as any girl next door. Her mother was a photographer. Her father was in advertising. Today, her net worth is $9 million dollars. "Anyone can be me," Sophia believes. "Work hard for yourself. Work smart. Bake in your social impact from the beginning. Put out positive and positive will come back to you.'

"We live in a world where it isn't always easy to find positive. We live in a society of put downs rather than build ups. It is important to be your own cheerleader, build yourself up and make your life what you deserve it to be. You can make a lot of money, or you can be rich. Which do you choose?"

1. Sophia Bush is many things but not
   a. an actress.
   b. a business owner.
   c. an investor.
   d. billionaire.

2. Sophia Bush has a

   _____
   relationship with money.
   a. strange
   b. bad
   c. positive
   d. worrisome

3. Who does Sophia believe you should work hard for
   a. yourself.
   b. her.
   c. your investors.
   d. your parents.

4. According to the passage, "It is important to be
   a. strong.
   b. your own cheerleader.
   c. into hotels and cars.
   d. focused.

5. Write the main idea of the reading in complete sentences.
   _____
   _____
   _____
   _____
   _____
   _____
   _____

Name: _____

Making A Lot of Money vs. Being Rich: Sophia Bush

Sophia Bush is a lot of things. Sophia Bush is an actress. Sophia Bush is an investor.	17
Sophia Bush is also the co-founder of Detroit Blows. Detroit Blows is a beauty salon in	34
Detroit that uses non-toxic products, but that is not the point. What is the point? You	51
can make a lot of money working a job, but it is rare to become rich unless you own	70
part or all of a business. That is a motto Sophia lives by.	83
"I have a positive relationship with money. I focus on what I have. On what I can	100
do. It is too easy to fear money. I think that having a positive relationship is	116
necessary. I think working hard is necessary. Put those two together and you can do	131
anything."	132
Sophia, started as any girl next door. Her mother was a photographer. Her father	146
was in advertising. Today, her net worth is $9 million dollars. "Anyone can be me,"	161
Sophia believes. "Work hard for yourself. Work smart. Bake in your social impact from	175
the beginning. Put out positive and positive will come back to you.'	187
"We live in a world where it isn't always easy to find positive. We live in a society of	206
put downs rather than build ups. It is important to be your own cheerleader, build	221
yourself up and make your life what you deserve it to be. You can make a lot of	239
money, or you can be rich. Which do you choose?"	249

Words Read:	Words Read:	Words Read:
minus mistakes:	minus mistakes:	minus mistakes:
equals wpms:	equals wpms:	equals wpms:

Name: _____

Chadwick Boseman

Born: November 29, 1976

Birthplace: Anderson, South Carolina

Occupation: Actor

College: Howard University; British American Drama Academy

Degree: Bachelor of Fine Arts

Died: August 28, 2020

Best Known For: Role of Marvel's Black Panther

He studied at Oxford. He won a Screen Actor's Guild Award. He won the NAACP Image Award. You may know him as the Black Panther. He is Chadwick Boseman.

Chadwick was born in Anderson, South Carolina. His mother was a nurse. His father worked in a cloth factory. Chadwick caught the acting bug in High School. He went to Howard University. By the end of college, Chadwick wanted to direct and write, only his acting career took off first.

Chadwick acted for many years before landing his first leading role. It was in the 2013 film 42. In the film, Chadwick played Jackie Robinson. In 2016, Chadwick was cast as Marvel's Black Panther. As part of the Marvel world, his career took off.

In the prime of his life, Chadwick was diagnosed with colon cancer. When he was diagnosed, his cancer was stage III. In 2020, it progressed to stage IV. He never spoke publicly about his cancer. On August 28, 2020, colon cancer took his life.

His family tweeted his death announcement. That tweet became the most-liked tweet ever. A mourner tweeted back: "The true power of Chadwick Boseman was bigger than anything we saw on screen...he inspired generations and showed them they can be anything they want – even superheroes."

1. Chadwick Boseman did all of the following except
   a. play the Black Panther in a movie.
   b. win an NAACP Imagine Award
   c. play Jackie Robinson in a movie.
   d. not go to Howard University

2. What was Chadwick Boseman's first leading role?
   a. Batman
   b. the Black Panther
   c. Jackie Robinson
   d. Howard

3. According to the reading, in the prime of his life, Chadwick Boseman
   a. played the Black Panther.
   b. won an NCAA award.
   c. was diagnosed with cancer.
   d. graduated from Howard University.

4. Chadwick Boseman died
   a. of a colon infection
   b. on August 29.
   c. on August 28.
   d. in South Carolina.

5. Write the main idea of the reading in complete sentences.

   _____

   _____

   _____

   _____

   _____

   _____

Name: _____

Chadwick Boseman

He studied at Oxford. He won a Screen Actor's Guild Award. He won the NAACP 15
Image Award. You may know him as the Black Panther. He is Chadwick Boseman. 29

Chadwick was born in Anderson, South Carolina. His mother was a nurse. His father 43
worked in a cloth factory. Chadwick caught the acting bug in High School. He went to 59
Howard University. By the end of college, Chadwick wanted to direct and write, only 73
his acting career took off first. 79

Chadwick acted for many years before landing his first leading role. It was in the 94
2013 film 42. In the film, Chadwick played Jackie Robinson. In 2016, Chadwick was 108
cast as Marvel's Black Panther. As part of the Marvel world, his career took off. 123

In the prime of his life, Chadwick was diagnosed with colon cancer. When he was 138
diagnosed, his cancer was stage III. In 2020, it progressed to stage IV. He never 153
spoke publicly about his cancer. On August 28, 2020, colon cancer took his life. 167

His family tweeted his death announcement. That tweet became the most-liked 179
tweet ever. A mourner tweeted back: "The true power of Chadwick Boseman was 192
bigger than anything we saw on screen…he inspired generations and showed them 205
they can be anything they want – even superheroes." 213

Words Read:	Words Read:	Words Read:
minus mistakes:	minus mistakes:	minus mistakes:
equals wpms:	equals wpms:	equals wpms:

Name: _____

Black Panther (Marvel Comics)

Black Panther is a comic book character. Black Panther is a superhero. Black Panther is a Marvel superhero. Black Panther was created by Stan Lee and Jack Kirby. Black Panther first appeared in the comic book **Fantastic Four #52.**

Black Panther's real name is T'Challa. He is the king of a fictional African nation. Black Panther's powers come from different places. Part of his powers come from drinking a heart-shaped herb. The rest come from his study of science, training, and hand-to-hand combat skills.

Black Panther is the first African superhero. There have been many films, television shows, and video games about Black Panther. The most recent movie of Black Panther stars Chadwick Boseman.

Black Panther wasn't always called Black Panther. In February 1972, Marvel tried using the name Black Leopard. That didn't last very long.

Marvel's first graphic novel was about the Black Panther. The story ran through 13 issues of Panther's Rage. Some critics call the text one of the best multi-hero epics ever. The story has also been called nearly-flawless.

Black Panther is now different than the original. He is a member of the *Ultimate's*.

1. Black Panther first appeared in?
    a. the Ultimate's
    b. the Fantastic Four
    c. Panther's Rage
    d. Marvel Team

2. The Black Panther was the first
    _____
    superhero.
    a. Marvel
    b. African
    c. comic book
    d. panther

3. For a brief time in the 1970s, the Black Panther was called
    a. Fantastic Four
    b. Panther
    c. Black Leopard
    d. the Ultimate Black Panther

4. Black Panther's real name is
    a. Chadwick Boseman
    b. T'Challa
    c. Jack Kirby
    d. Stan Lee

5. Write the main idea of the reading in complete sentences.

    _____
    _____
    _____
    _____
    _____
    _____
    _____
    _____

Black Panther (Marvel Comics)

Black Panther is a comic book character. Black Panther is a superhero. Black	13
Panther is a Marvel superhero. Black Panther was created by Stan Lee and Jack Kirby.	28
Black Panther first appeared in the comic book Fantastic Four #52.	39
Black Panther's real name is T'Challa. He is the king of a fictional African nation.	54
Black Panther's powers come from different places. Part of his powers come from	67
drinking a heart-shaped herb. The rest come from his study of science, training, and	82
hand-to-hand combat skills.	87
Black Panther is the first African superhero. There have been many films, television	100
shows, and video games about Black Panther. The most recent movie of Black Panther	114
stars Chadwick Boseman.	117
Black Panther wasn't always called Black Panther. In February 1972, Marvel tried	129
using the name Black Leopard. That didn't last very long.	139
Marvel's first graphic novel was about the Black Panther. The story ran through 13	153
issues of Panther's Rage. Some critics call the text one of the best multi-hero epics	169
ever. The story has also been called nearly-flawless.	178
Black Panther is now different than the original. He is a member of the *Ultimate's*.	193

Words Read:	Words Read:	Words Read:
minus mistakes:	minus mistakes:	minus mistakes:
equals wpms:	equals wpms:	equals wpms:

Spider-Man – The Most Popular of All-Time

Is Spider-Man the most popular Marvel Superhero of all time? Some say he is. Spider-Man is one of the best-known superheroes around. He is also one of the best loved.

Spider-man was created by Stan Lee and Steve Ditko. Spidey first appeared in a comic book series called *Amazing Fantasy*. He came out in edition #15. The year was 1962. The era was considered the Silver Age of Comic Books. Since then, Spider-Man has been in countless comics. Spider-Man has been in numerous television shows. He has also starred in movies and video games - too many to mention.

Spider-man's human name is Peter Parker. Peter is an orphan. He was raised by his Aunt May and Uncle Ben. He was raised in New York City. Spider-Man's writers had him struggle with adolescence. He was also poor.

Spider-Man's abilities came after a bite from a radioactive spider. The bite changed Peter. He can now cling to surfaces. He has superhuman strength. He has "spider-sense" as well. This "spider-sense" enables Spider-Man to know when danger is lurking.

Spider-Man was rejected and lonely as a teen. He learned everything without a mentor or a sidekick. This made him more relatable. It wasn't long before Spidey was a fan favorite. Spider-Man is so loved that he just may be the most popular superhero of all time.

1. Who created Spider-Man?
   a. Stan Lee and Steve Ditko
   b. Peter Parker and Stan Lee
   c. Peter Parker and Steve Ditko
   d. Steve Lee and Peter Parker

2. Spider-Man made his comic appearance in
   a. the Golden Age of Comics
   b. a series called *Amazing Fantasy*
   c. a series called *Fantastic Four*
   d. the DC comic *Amazing Spider-Man*

3. What was Spider-Man's childhood like?
   a. he was poor and lonely
   b. he was rich and athletic
   c. he was poor and an orphan
   d. he was poor and happy

4. What does Spider-Man's "spider-sense" do?
   a. helps Spider-Man climb walls
   b. helps Spider-Man detect danger
   c. helps Spider-Man weave webs
   d. helps Spider-Man become the most popular superhero of all time

5. Write the main idea of the reading in complete sentences.

   _____

   _____

   _____

   _____

   _____

Spider-Man: The Most Popular Superhero of All Time

Is Spider-Man the most popular Marvel Superhero of all time? Some say he is.	15
Spider-Man is one of the best-known superheroes around. He is also one of the best	32
loved.	33
Spider-man was created by Stan Lee and Steve Ditko. Spidey first appeared in a	47
comic book series called *Amazing Fantasy*. He came out in edition #15. The year was	62
1962. The era was considered the Silver Age of Comic Books. Since then, Spider-Man	77
has been in countless comics. Spider-Man has been in numerous television shows. He	91
has also starred in movies and video games - too many to mention.	103
Spider-man's human name is Peter Parker. Peter is an orphan. He was raised by his	119
Aunt May and Uncle Ben. He was raised in New York City. Spider-Man's writers had	135
him struggle with adolescence. He was also poor.	143
Spider-Man's abilities came after a bite from a radioactive spider. The bite	156
changed Peter. He can now cling to surfaces. He has superhuman strength. He has	170
"spider-sense" as well. This "spider-sense" enables Spider-Man to know when danger is	184
lurking.	185
Spider-Man was rejected and lonely as a teen. He learned everything without a	199
mentor or a sidekick. This made him more relatable. It wasn't long before Spidey was	214
a fan favorite. Spider-Man is so loved that he just may be the most popular superhero	231
of all time.	234

Words Read:	Words Read:	Words Read:
minus mistakes:	minus mistakes:	minus mistakes:
equals wpms:	equals wpms:	equals wpms:

Name: _____

Katniss Everdeen

Katniss Everdeen. The Hunger Games. Not the movie. The book. It has to be the book. If you want to know the real Katniss, you must read the book. Straight black hair, olive skin, and grey eyes. She's from the poorest section of District 12. She is bold. She is courageous. She is smart. She enjoys being alone. She is described as a turtle.

Katniss can hunt. She can trap. She is as skilled as her father who died when she was younger. She is the sole provider of her family. She's been the provider since she was eleven. Hunting, however, is illegal in Katniss' world. It is punishable by death. Katniss does it anyway. She must feed her family. Maybe she is a little rebellious. She and her family eat what she catches. If there are leftovers, she sells them on the black market. There is that rebellious spirit again.

Katniss is a bold and caring person. She is a fictional character whose traits don't really change. Never during the novel does Katniss lose her identity. Never does she lose the honesty that drives her. She is good and pure. That does not change even when the world around her does. Even when she is thrust into unthinkable circumstances, Katniss remains the same.

Katniss Everdeen. May the odds be ever in her favor. If you don't know what that means, read The Hunger Games.

1. Which of the below is not one of Katniss Everdeen's character traits?
   a. intelligent
   b. brave
   c. talkative
   d. rebellious

2. Katniss has taken care of her family since the age of
   a. twelve
   b. eleven
   c. sixteen
   d. eighteen

3. Katniss Everdeen is
   a. a fictional character
   b. a hunter
   c. a gatherer
   d. all of the above

4. Why does Katniss hunt when it is illegal?
   a. she is rebellious
   b. she likes to hunt
   c. she must feed her family
   d. she likes to sell on the black market

5. Write the main idea of the reading in complete sentences.

_____

_____

_____

_____

_____

_____

_____

Katniss Everdeen

Katniss Everdeen. The Hunger Games. Not the movie. The book. It has to be the	15
book. If you want to know the real Katniss, you must read the book. Straight black	31
hair, olive skin, and grey eyes. She's from the poorest section of District 12. She is bold.	48
She is courageous. She is smart. She enjoys being alone. She is described as a turtle.	64
Katniss can hunt. She can trap. She is as skilled as her father who died when she	81
was younger. She is the sole provider of her family. She's been the provider since she	97
was eleven. Hunting, however, is illegal in Katniss' world. It is punishable by death.	111
Katniss does it anyway. She must feed her family. Maybe she is a little rebellious. She	127
and her family eat what she catches. If there are leftovers, she sells them on the black	144
market. There is that rebellious spirit again.	151
Katniss is a bold and caring person. She is a fictional character whose traits don't	166
really change. Never during the novel does Katniss lose her identity. Never does she	180
lose the honesty that drives her. She is good and pure. That does not change even	196
when the world around her does. Even when she is thrust into unthinkable	209
circumstances, Katniss remains the same.	214
Katniss Everdeen. May the odds be ever in her favor. If you don't know what that	230
means, read The Hunger Games.	235

Words Read:	Words Read:	Words Read:
minus mistakes:	minus mistakes:	minus mistakes:
equals wpms:	equals wpms:	equals wpms:

Name: _____

Veronica Roth

Born: August 19, 1988
Birthplace: New York, New York
Occupation: Writer
College: Northwestern University
Best Known For: The Divergent Series

Veronica Roth is an American novelist. She created the popular <u>Divergent</u> series. Roth grew up in Illinois. As a child, she loved reading. One of her favorite books was <u>The Giver</u>. <u>The Giver</u> is a dystopian novel by Lois Lowry. It is no wonder <u>Divergent</u> is dystopian as well.

Roth was a college student when she wrote the first book of the series. She wrote the entire book over winter break during her senior year at Northwestern. That was in 2010. In March of the same year, Roth took her manuscript to a writers' conference. She found an agent. Within a month, the novel was sold to Harper Collins.

<u>Divergent</u> was released in 2011. It came out as number six on the *New York Times* bestsellers list. The second book in the series was released the next year. <u>Insurgent</u> was its title. Book two captured the number one spot on the *New York Times* bestsellers list.

Roth found her place quickly. Her books came on the heels of the popular <u>Twilight</u> and <u>Hunger Games</u> series. Roth's fan base grew quickly. By the time the third book in the series was ready to go - it became the most pre-ordered book ever.

Roth has penned eight books since the <u>Divergent</u> series debuted.

1. The second book in the <u>Divergent</u> series is title
   a. <u>Allegiant</u>
   b. <u>Divergent II</u>
   c. <u>Insurgent</u>
   d. <u>Hunger Games</u>

2. <u>Divergent</u> debuted on the New York Times Bestsellers list at
   a. number one
   b. number two
   c. number six
   d. number seven

3. Victoria Roth was born in
   a. Illinois
   b. the northwest
   c. New York State
   d. New York City, New York

4. What was one of Roth's favorite books as a child?
   a. <u>Divergent</u>
   b. <u>Twilight</u>
   c. <u>The Giver</u>
   d. <u>Insurgent</u>

5. Write the main idea of the reading in complete sentences.

_____

_____

_____

_____

_____

_____

_____

_____

Name: _____

Veronica Roth

Veronica Roth is an American novelist. She created the popular <u>Divergent</u> series.   12
Roth grew up in Illinois. As a child, she loved reading. One of her favorite books was   29
<u>The Giver</u>. <u>The Giver</u> is a dystopian novel by Lois Lowry. It is no wonder <u>Divergent</u> is   46
dystopian as well.   49

Roth was a college student when she wrote the first book of the series. She wrote   65
the entire book over winter break during her senior year at Northwestern. That was in   80
2010. In March of the same year, Roth took her manuscript to a writers' conference.   95
She found an agent. Within a month, the novel was sold to Harper Collins.   109

<u>Divergent</u> was released in 2011. It came out as number six on the *New York Times*   125
bestsellers list. The second book in the series was released the next year. <u>Insurgent</u>   139
was its title. Book two captured the number one spot on the *New York Times*   154
bestsellers list.   156

Roth found her place quickly. Her books came on the heels of the popular <u>Twilight</u>   171
and <u>Hunger Games</u> series. Roth's fan base grew quickly. By the time the third book in   187
the series was ready to go – it became the most pre-ordered book ever.   201

Roth has penned eight books since the <u>Divergent</u> series debuted.   211

Words Read:	Words Read:	Words Read:
minus mistakes:	minus mistakes:	minus mistakes:
equals wpms:	equals wpms:	equals wpms:

Name: _____

Danny Duncan

Born: July 27, 1992
Birthplace: Englewood, Florida
Lives Now: Los Angeles, California
Occupation: YouTube
Best Known For: Skateboard Videos

Danny Duncan is a YouTube star. He is a social media influencer. He is a skateboarder. He is known for his YouTube channel post "Prank." He is also known for his skateboard videos. His YouTube channel has more than 3 million subscribers.

Danny did not have much money growing up. Raised by his mother, Danny did not go to college. On March 6, 2014, Danny started a YouTube channel. Some of his most watched videos are "Going Down a Ladder on an Hoverboard" and "Hot Tub in the Freeway."

Making YouTube videos is not easy work. Being an influencer makes Danny money, but not as much as many people think. "While $720 dollars a day is a lot of money. It isn't millions per year – like many people think," Danny said in a 2018 interview. Danny would like to be an actor. He is using YouTube as a platform to begin his career.

Duncan is close to his family. After a prank video about dumping pennies, Duncan posted a video "Surprising My Sister With a New Car." In the video, Danny drowns his sister's old car. Then, he surprises her with a new one.

In 2019, Danny started a line of clothing. The line is available at Zumiez. His clothing line makes him way more money than his videos do.

1. Danny is all of the following except
   a. a social influencer.
   b. a skateboarder.
   c. a Rockstar.
   d. a clothing line owner and promoter.

2. Danny Duncan started his YouTube channel on
   a. March 6, 2014.
   b. July 27, 1992.
   c. September 7, 2019.
   d. January 27, 2914.

3. Danny Duncan lives in
   a. Englewood, Florida
   b. Los Angeles, California
   c. Coldwater, Florida
   d. Clearwater, California

4. After posting a prank video about pennies, Danny
   a. gave his sister a car.
   b. gave his mother a car.
   c. gave his sister a house.
   d. gave his mother a house.

5. Write the main idea of the reading in complete sentences.

   _____

   _____

   _____

   _____

   _____

   _____

   _____

Name: _____

Danny Duncan

Danny Duncan is a YouTube star. He is a social media influencer. He is a | 15
skateboarder. He is known for his YouTube channel post "Prank." He is also known for | 30
his skateboard videos. His YouTube channel has more than 3 million subscribers. | 42

Danny did not have much money growing up. Raised by his mother, Danny did not | 57
go to college. On March 6, 2014, Danny started a YouTube channel. Some of his most | 73
watched videos are "Going Down a Ladder on an Hoverboard" and "Hot Tub in the | 88
Freeway." | 89

Making YouTube videos is not easy work. Being an influencer makes Danny money, | 102
but not as much as many people think. "While $720 dollars a day is a lot of money. It | 121
isn't millions per year – like many people think," Danny said in a 2018 interview. Danny | 136
would like to be an actor. He is using YouTube as a platform to begin his career. | 153

Duncan is close to his family. After a prank video about dumping pennies, Duncan | 167
posted a video "Surprising My Sister With a New Car." In the video, Danny drowns his | 183
sister's old car. Then, he surprises her with a new one. | 194

In 2019, Danny started a line of clothing. The line is available at Zumiez. His clothing | 210
line makes him way more money than his videos do. | 220

Words Read:	Words Read:	Words Read:
minus mistakes:	minus mistakes:	minus mistakes:
equals wpms:	equals wpms:	equals wpms:

Name: _____

Emma Chamberlain

Born: May 22, 2001
Birthplace: San Bruno, California
Lives Now: West Hollywood, California
Occupation: YouTube Star
Known For: Making YouTube Videos

Lists: People Magazine 25 Most Influential People on the Internet **and** Time Magazines 100 Next List

Emma Chamberlain is a social media star. She is a YouTube star. She has 8.5 million subscribers. Emma's first posts were about her life. She posted about life. She posted about being a teen. Just being herself is something other teens can relate to.

Emma is an only child. Her parents divorced when she was five. But she is close to both. Emma uploaded her first video on June 2, 2017. During that summer, she posted almost everyday. After almost two months of posting, Emma only had 50 followers. On July 27, 2017, she posted a video *We All Owe The Dollar Store An Apology*. The video went viral.

In August, Emma's channel quickly gained subscribers. From August 1 to August 31, Emma went from having 4,000 followers to having 150,000 followers. From September 2017 to June 2019, the vlogger gained 100,000 subscribers per month.

In 2018, Emma and the shopping app Dote released a line of clothing. Emma designed a line called *Low Key/High Key by Emma*. The line was short lived. Emma broke with the app in 2018 because of Dote's alleged treatment of racial minorities.

Emma moved to Los Angeles. She's been working with other influencers. Emma has paired with brands like Louis Vuitton. She's also paired with Calvin Klein. She has worked with Vogue and Cosmo. She has been called "the most popular girl in the world." And, well, Emma Chamberlain just may be – the most popular girl in the world.

1. How many subscribers does Emma Chamberlain's YouTube channel have?
   a. 8.5 million
   b. 4,000
   c. 150,000
   d. over a million

2. Emma's first video to go viral was
   a. Diary of an American Teen
   b. We All Owe the Dollar Store an Apology
   c. Low Key/High Key by Emma
   d. The Most Popular Girl in the World

3. Emma has paired with each of the following brands except
   a. Calvin Klein
   b. Dote
   c. Louie Calvin
   d. Louie Vuitton

4. During her first two months on YouTube, Emma had
   a. 50 followers
   b. 150,000 followers
   c. 8.5 million followers
   d. 4,000 followers

5. Write the main idea of the reading in complete sentences.

_____

_____

_____

_____

_____

_____

_____

_____

Emma Chamberlain

Emma Chamberlain is a social media star. She is a YouTube star. She has 8.5 million | 16
subscribers. Emma's first posts were about her life. She posted about life. She posted | 30
about being a teen. Just being herself is something other teens can relate to. | 44

Emma is an only child. Her parents divorced when she was five. But she is close to | 61
both. Emma uploaded her first video on June 2, 2017. During that summer, she posted | 76
almost everyday. After almost two months of posting, Emma only had 50 followers. On | 90
July 27, 2017, she posted a video *We All Owe The Dollar Store An Apology*. The video | 107
went viral. | 109

In August, Emma's channel quickly gained subscribers. From August 1 to August 31, | 122
Emma went from having 4,000 followers to having 150,000 followers. From September | 134
2017 to June 2019, the vlogger gained 100,000 subscribers per month. | 145

In 2018, Emma and the shopping app Dote released a line of clothing. Emma | 159
designed a line called *Low Key/High Key by Emma*. The line was short lived. Emma | 175
broke with the app in 2018 because of Dote's alleged treatment of racial minorities. | 189

Emma moved to Los Angeles. She's been working with other influencers. Emma has | 202
paired with brands like Louis Vuitton. She's also paired with Calvin Klein. She has | 216
worked with Vogue and Cosmo. She has been called "the most popular girl in the | 231
world." And, well, Emma Chamberlain just may be – the most popular girl in the world. | 246

Words Read:	Words Read:	Words Read:
minus mistakes:	minus mistakes:	minus mistakes:
equals wpms:	equals wpms:	equals wpms:

Name: _____

Nike

One of Nike's latest shoes is Nike Air Force 1. The kicker - this "new" shoe has been around since 1982. The difference? In 1982, they did not cost $90.

"Air in a box," read the original ad. The Air Force 1 was the first basketball shoe to have air in its heel. Back then, Nike was new to basketball. The company's roots were running. Running shoes and basketball shoes are not alike at all. Running is heel-toe. It is a straight-line sport. In Basketball, there are cuts. There is jumping and landing. Heavy landing. Very heavy landing.

To hook the basketball market, Nike signed six NBA players to wear their shoes. The original six, in 1982, included Moses Malone and Bobby Jones. Nike stopped making the original Air Force 1 in 1984, but people still wanted them. Demand was high. Stores began asking Nike to make the shoe again. This is common now. Back in 1982, it never happened.

Nike didn't think people would buy a shoe that was "old." In 1986, Nike changed their mind. They made the Air Force 1 again and again and again. Today, there are over 2,000 versions of the shoe. It is still going strong.

Have you ever owned a pair?

1. Nike's latest shoe was developed in
   a. 2020
   b. 2019
   c. 1982
   d. last September

2. Nike shoes were originally designed for
   a. runners
   b. basketball players
   c. tennis players
   d. football players

3. To market basketball shoes Nike hired _____ and _____ to wear them on the courts.
   a. Bobby Jones and Moses Malone
   b. the Air Force
   c. Bobby Jones and Michael Jordan
   d. Moses Malone and Charles Barkley

4. Nike brought the Air force 1 shoe back because
   a. it was the norm to recycle shoe designs
   b. stores said demand was high
   c. Bobby Jones wanted to wear them on the court
   d. the didn't – Air Force 1 is now retired

5. Write the main idea of the reading in complete sentences.

_____

_____

_____

_____

_____

_____

_____

Nike

One of Nike's latest shoes is Nike Air Force 1. The kicker - this "new" shoe has been   17
around since 1982. The difference? In 1982, they did not cost $90.   29

"Air in a box," read the original ad. The Air Force 1 was the first basketball shoe to   47
have air in its heel. Back then, Nike was new to basketball. The company's roots were   63
running. Running shoes and basketball shoes are not alike at all. Running is heel-toe. It   79
is a straight-line sport. In Basketball, there are cuts. There is jumping and landing.   94
Heavy landing. Very heavy landing.   99

To hook the basketball market, Nike signed six NBA players to wear their shoes. The   114
original six, in 1982, included Moses Malone and Bobby Jones. Nike stopped making   127
the original Air Force 1 in 1984, but people still wanted them. Demand was high. Stores   143
began asking Nike to make the shoe again. This is common now. Back in 1982, it never   160
happened.   161

Nike didn't think people would buy a shoe that was "old." In 1986, Nike changed   176
their mind. They made the Air Force 1 again and again and again. Today, there are   192
over 2,000 versions of the shoe. It is still going strong.   203

Have you ever owned a pair?   209

Words Read:	Words Read:	Words Read:
minus mistakes:	minus mistakes:	minus mistakes:
equals wpms:	equals wpms:	equals wpms:

Name: _____

LeBron James

Born: December 30, 1984
Birthplace: Akron, Ohio
Occupation: Basketball Player
High School: St. Vincent – St. Mary
Draft Pick: Round 1 – Number 1
Teams: Cleveland Cavaliers and Miami Heat
Best Known For: 6 ft 9 in
Weight: 250

LeBron James is a pro basketball player. He is considered one of the greatest basketball players of all time. James has helped his NBA teams play in eight NBA Finals. That would be eight final championship games in a row.

James has won three NBA championships. He was voted NBA MVP four times. (MVP means Most Valuable Player.) James was also voted MVP in three championship finals. James has even won two Olympic gold metals.

James holds the all-time record for playoff points. He is the third all-time point scorer in the history of the league. James has been selected All-NBA First Team twelve times; this is the all-time record. He's played in sixteen All-Star Games. He was selected All-Star MVP three times.

Lebron is one of the few NBA players who was drafted right out of high school. He is magical on the court. Lebron was also a great football player. He was named to the first team all-state football team when he was a sophomore in high school! His position was wide receiver.

Lebron's nickname is King James. He has a tattoo that reads "Chosen 1." Lebron was the youngest person ever to be drafted by the NBA at the age of 18. The combination of skill, strength, jumping ability, and height make him an unstoppable force and one of the best athletes in the world.

1. Lebron James has played for all of the following teams except
   a. Cleveland Cavaliers
   b. Miami Lakers
   c. Miami Heat
   d. St. Vincent-St. Mary

2. LeBron's tattoo says
   a. Number 1
   b. The King
   c. King James
   d. Chosen 1

3. Lebron won _____ Olympic gold metals.
   a. two
   b. four
   c. sixteen
   d. twelve

4. In high school, Lebron made all state first team for
   a. basketball
   b. football
   c. soccer
   d. basketball and football

5. Write the main idea of the reading in complete sentences.

   _____

   _____

   _____

   _____

   _____

   _____

   _____

LeBron James

LeBron James is a pro basketball player. He is considered one of the greatest   14
basketball players of all time. James has helped his NBA teams play in eight NBA   29
Finals. That would be eight final championship games in a row.   40

James has won three NBA championships. He was voted NBA MVP four times. (MVP   54
means Most Valuable Player.) James was also voted MVP in three championship finals.   67
James has even won two Olympic gold metals.   75

James holds the all-time record for playoff points. He is the third all-time point   91
scorer in the history of the league. James has been selected All-NBA First Team   106
twelve times; this is the all-time record. He's played in sixteen All-Star Games. He was   123
selected All-Star MVP three times.   129

Lebron is one of the few NBA players who was drafted right out of high school. He   146
is magical on the court. Lebron was also a great football player. He was named to the   163
first team all-state football team when he was a sophomore in high school! His position   179
was wide receiver.   182

Lebron's nickname is King James. He has a tattoo that reads "Chosen 1." Lebron   196
was the youngest person ever to be drafted by the NBA at the age of 18. The   213
combination of skill, strength, jumping ability, and height make him an unstoppable   225
force and one of the best athletes in the world.   235

Words Read:	Words Read:	Words Read:
minus mistakes:	minus mistakes:	minus mistakes:
equals wpms:	equals wpms:	equals wpms:

Name: _____

Joan of Arc – Part 1

Born: 1412
Birthplace: Domremy, France
Occupation: Military Leader
Died: May 30, 1431, in Rouen, France
Best Known For: Leading the French against the English in the Hundred Years War

Photo: Joan of Arc, historiated initial from Archives Nationales, Paris, AE II 2490. Public domain.

Joan of Arc grew up in a small town in France. Her father was a farmer. He also worked as an official in their small town. Joan worked on the farm with her father. Joan also worked in the house with her mother. Joan learned to sew and cook. She also studied religion.

When Joan was around twelve-years-old she had a vision. She saw Michael the Archangel. The Archangel told her she was to lead the French. He told her she was to lead the French in a battle against the English.

Joan continued to have visions and hear voices for years. France was very religious. Joan was very religious. Joan said her voices were beautiful visions from God. When Joan was sixteen, she made the decision to listen to the visions.

Joan was a peasant - a farm girl. Where in the world was she going to get an army? How was she ever going to defeat the English? She decided to go to ask the king of France for an army. She made it as far as a commander before she was stopped. The king laughed at little Joan.

Joan did not give up. Finally, she got support from the local leaders. She met the king. The king figured he had nothing to lose. He gave Joan an army.

Joan was an inspirational leader. Eventually, Joan and the French Army caused the English troops to retreat from Orleans. She won a great victory and saved the French.

1. What was special about Joan of Arc?
   a. Joan was a military leader as a young lady
   b. Joan had visions
   c. Joan led the French to victory in the Battle of Orleans
   d. all the above

2. Joan's visions told her to
   a. help her mother and father work the farm
   b. learn religion and go out and help people
   c. that she was going to meet the king
   d. that she was going to lead the French in a battle against English

3. According to the reading, Joan was a _____ leader
   a. protected
   b. harsh
   c. inspirational
   d. quiet but effective

4. Joan's first vision was from
   a. Michael, the Archangel
   b. God
   c. Gabriel, the Archangel
   d. God and Michael, the Archangel

5. Write the main idea of the reading in complete sentences.

_____

_____

_____

_____

_____

Joan of Arc - Part 1

Joan of Arc grew up in a small town in France. Her father was a farmer. He also	18
worked as an official in their small town. Joan worked on the farm with her father.	34
Joan also worked in the house with her mother. Joan learned to sew and cook. She	50
also studied religion.	53
When Joan was around twelve-years-old she had a vision. She saw Michael the	68
Archangel. The Archangel told her she was to lead the French. He told her she was to	85
lead the French in a battle against the English.	94
Joan continued to have visions and hear voices for years. France was very religious.	108
Joan was very religious. Joan said her voices were beautiful visions from God. When	122
Joan was sixteen, she made the decision to listen to the visions.	134
Joan was a peasant - a farm girl. Where in the world was she going to get an army?	152
How was she ever going to defeat the English? She decided to go to ask the king of	170
France for an army. She made it as far as a commander before she was stopped. The	187
king laughed at little Joan.	192
Joan did not give up. Finally, she got support from the local leaders. She met the	208
king. The king figured he had nothing to lose. He gave Joan an army.	222
Joan was an inspirational leader. Eventually, Joan and the French Army caused the	235
English troops to retreat from Orleans. She won a great victory and saved the French.	250

Words Read:	Words Read:	Words Read:
minus mistakes:	minus mistakes:	minus mistakes:
equals wpms:	equals wpms:	equals wpms:

Name: _____

Joan of Arc – Part 2

Facts:
- When the king first met Joan, he dressed as a courtier to try and fool her. She was not fooled.
- Joan cut her hair to look more like a man.
- Joan helped King Charles regain his crown, but King Charles did nothing to help Joan once she was captured.
- Joan's nickname was "The Maid of Orleans.
- Joan was made a Catholic saint in 1920.

Photo: Joan of Arc, historiated initial from Archives Nationales, Paris. Public domain.

Imagine being eighteen-years-old and leading an army to victory. Imagine being a young lady, in 1412, leading an army to victory.

So, Joan wins the Battle of Orleans. But only half of her vision had come true. She needed to lead King Charles to the city of Rheims to be crowned king. True to the vision, Joan escorted Charles to Rheims. There, Charles was crowned king.

Joan heard another city was under attack. She took a small army and went to help the city. Joan was captured by the English. She was taken to England. The English gave her a trial. The trial was to prove that she was anti-god. They questioned Joan. They questioned Joan for days and days. They were looking for anything she had done that deserved death.

What did they find? Nothing, except that Joan had dressed as a man. They said that was enough to sentence Joan to death.

Joan of Arc was burned alive at the stake. She asked for a cross before she died. An English soldier gave her a small wooden cross. It is said, Joan forgave her accusers before she died. She was only nineteen-years-old at the time.

1. What battle did Joan win?
   a. Protestant
   b. Orleans
   c. Saratoga
   d. Paris, France

2. Who captured Joan?
   a. the French
   b. King Charles
   c. Orleans
   d. the English

3. What were the charges that caused Joan to be put to death?
   a. she was against God
   b. she was a female soldie
   c. she was a prisoner of war
   d. she dressed like a man

4. Who gave Joan a wooden cross before she died
   a. an English soldier
   b. a French soldier
   c. the King
   d. a Catholic saint

5. Write the main idea of the reading in complete sentences

_____

_____

_____

_____

_____

_____

Joan of Arc - Part 2

Imagine being eighteen-years-old and leading an army to victory. Imagine being a	14
young lady, in 1412, leading an army to victory.	23
So, Joan wins the Battle of Orleans. But only half of her vision had come true. She	40
needed to lead King Charles to the city of Rheims to be crowned king. True to the	57
vision, Joan escorted Charles to Rheims. There, Charles was crowned king.	68
Joan heard another city was under attack. She took a small army and went to help	84
the city. Joan was captured by the English. She was taken to England. The English	99
gave her a trial. The trial was to prove that she was anti-god. They questioned Joan.	116
They questioned Joan for days and days. They were looking for anything she had	130
done that deserved death.	134
What did they find? Nothing, except that Joan had dressed as a man. They said	149
that was enough to sentence Joan to death.	157
Joan of Arc was burned alive at the stake. She asked for a cross before she died.	174
An English soldier gave her a small wooden cross. It is said, Joan forgave her accusers	190
before she died. She was only nineteen-years-old at the time.	202

Words Read:	Words Read:	Words Read:
minus mistakes:	minus mistakes:	minus mistakes:
equals wpms:	equals wpms:	equals wpms:

Name: _____

Wonder Woman

Publisher: DC Comics
First Appearance: All Star Comics #8
Release Date: 1941
Created by: William Moulton Marston and H.G. Peter
Alter Egos: Princess Diana of Themyscira and Diana Prince
Species: Amazon Goddess

Public Domain

Wonder Women was created during World War II. Wonder Woman's original storyline: Wonder Woman takes on Axis military forces. Oh, and also a few supervillains. Over time, her storyline became more personal. It focused more on her backstory. Her backstory is Greek mythology.

During the 1940s, female storylines were "damsels in distress." Wonder Woman was anything but a damsel in distress. Wonder Woman was a force. She even rescued herself out of her own bondage.

Wonder Woman was created by a feminist. She was created in the Golden Age of Comic Books. In the 1940s, Wonder Woman belonged to the Justice Society of America. Later, she belonged to the Justice League.

Wonder Woman Facts:

- Wonder Woman was an instant sensation.
- She has never worn a skirt or dress.
- The man who created the Wonder Woman character also invented the lie detector test.
- Wonder Woman was originally made in clay. The storyline is that her mother, Queen Hippolyta, made her of clay. Then her mother brought her to life.
- Wonder Woman's alter ego, Diana Prince, has held many jobs. She's worked in fast food, as a military secretary, as a romance writer, and as a singer.

1. Wonder Woman has held many jobs, but she was never a
   a. romance writer
   b. fast food worker
   c. military secretary
   d. dancer

2. The first Wonder Woman comics were centered around
   a. World War I
   b. World War II
   c. The Amazon
   d. Greek Mythology

3. What was Wonder Woman originally made from?
   a. her mother
   b. flesh and bones
   c. water
   d. clay

4. Which of the following is not a Wonder Woman fact
   a. the creator of Wonder Woman also created the lie detector
   b. the creator of Wonder Woman also created the blender
   c. Wonder Woman is also Diana Prince
   d. Wonder Woman was part of the Justice Society of America

5. Write the main idea of the reading in complete sentences.

   _____

   _____

   _____

   _____

Wonder Woman

Wonder Women was created during World War II. Wonder Woman's original	11
storyline: Wonder Woman takes on Axis military forces. Oh, and also a few	24
supervillains. Over time, her storyline became more personal. It focused more on her	37
backstory. Her backstory is Greek mythology.	43
During the 1940s, female storylines were "damsels in distress." Wonder Woman was	55
anything but a damsel in distress. Wonder Woman was a force. She even rescued	69
herself out of her own bondage.	75
Wonder Woman was created by a feminist. She was created in the Golden Age of	90
Comic Books. In the 1940s, Wonder Woman belonged to the Justice Society of	103
America. Later, she belonged to the Justice League.	111

Wonder Woman Facts:

- Wonder Woman was an instant sensation.
- She has never worn a skirt or dress.
- The man who created the Wonder Woman character also invented the lie detector test.
- Wonder Woman was originally made in clay. The storyline is that her mother, Queen Hippolyta, made her of clay. Then her mother brought her to life.
- Wonder Woman's alter ego, Diana Prince, has held many jobs. She's worked in fast food, as a military secretary, as a romance writer, and as a singer.

Wonder Woman Facts:	114
	120
	128
	140
	142
	155
	168
	181
	195

Words Read:	Words Read:	Words Read:
minus mistakes:	minus mistakes:	minus mistakes:
equals wpms:	equals wpms:	equals wpms:

Name: _____

Magic the Gathering

Author's image.

Magic the Gathering is a card game. It was created by Richard Garfield in 1993. Cards belonging to the original first three versions command upwards of $100,000 dollars each.

Magic is a trading card game. It is the most popular trading card game ever. There are about thirty-five million players worldwide. Over twenty billion Magic cards were made between 2008 and 2016. Many early cards are now retired. Creators of the game have promised not to remake some of them. This contributes to their value.

The coveted Alpha or Beta Black Lotus is a powerful and expensive card. One sold in May of 2019 for $166,000!

Each game of Magic is a battle between wizards. These wizards are known as planeswalkers. The wizards cast spells. They use artifacts and creatures to defeat their opponents. Traditionally, two players start with 20 life points. The first person left with lives at the end of the game is the winner.

New Magic cards are released annually. They are called expansion sets. There are professional Magic players. There are worldwide tournaments. Placing first in a Magic tournament could mean millions for the winner.

Magic combines luck and skill. Professional players complain there is too much luck involved. Others feel that luck is what makes the game fair for all players. Either way, Magic the Gathering is fun game to play and a lucrative one to collect.

1. The Black Lotus sold for
   a. $35
   b. $166
   c. $166,000
   d. $20

2. In Magic the Gathering, a wizard is called
   a. a wizard
   b. a planeswalker
   c. a black lotus
   d. an artifact

3. How popular is Magic the Gathering?
   a. it is popular enough to have tournaments
   b. it is the best-selling trading card game in the U.S.
   c. it is the most poplar trading card game ever
   d. the reading doesn't say

4. How many lives does a Magic player start with?
   a. 35
   b. 166
   c. one
   d. 20

5. Write the main idea of the reading in complete sentences.

   _____

   _____

   _____

   _____

   _____

   _____

Magic the Gathering

Magic the Gathering is a card game. It was created by Richard Garfield in 1993.	15
Cards belonging to the original first three versions command upwards of $100,000	27
dollars each.	29
Magic is a trading card game. It is the most popular trading card game ever. There	45
are about thirty-five million players worldwide. Over twenty billion Magic cards were	58
made between 2008 and 2016. Many early cards are now retired. Creators of the game	73
have promised not to remake some of them. This contributes to their value.	86
The coveted Alpha or Beta Black Lotus is a powerful and expensive card. One sold	101
in May of 2019 for $166,000!	107
Each game of Magic is a battle between wizards. These wizards are known as	121
planeswalkers. The wizards cast spells. They use artifacts and creatures to defeat their	134
opponents. Traditionally, two players start with 20 life points. The first person left with	148
lives at the end of the game is the winner.	158
New Magic cards are released annually. They are called expansion sets. There are	171
professional Magic players. There are worldwide tournaments. Placing first in a Magic	183
tournament could mean millions for the winner.	190
Magic combines luck and skill. Professional players complain there is too much luck	203
involved. Others feel that luck is what makes the game fair for all players. Either way,	219
Magic the Gathering is fun game to play and a lucrative one to collect.	233

Words Read:	Words Read:	Words Read:
minus mistakes:	minus mistakes:	minus mistakes:
equals wpms:	equals wpms:	equals wpms:

Name: _____

Six Flags

Author's image.

Six Flags is a company that runs amusement parks. Six Flags was established in 1961. Today, it is the largest theme park owner on earth. Six Flags has 19 parks. The parks are in the U.S., Mexico, and Canada. The parks are not for the faint of heart. Six Flags facts:

1. Six Flags sells over 15,000 funnel cakes daily. Fifteen thousand! Everyday!

2. Six Flags owns over 800 rides. One hundred twenty of them are roller coasters. Many of the highest and fastest roller coasters in the world are owned by Six Flags.

3. Six Flags Magic Mountain is in Valencia, California. It is the **Roller Coaster Capitol of the World**. Home to 18 roller coasters – Magic Mountain has more coasters than any other park on earth.

4. More than 24 million people visit Six Flags parks each year.

5. Six Flags Magic Mountain is home to the world's tallest and fastest looping coaster. The coaster is called *Full Throttle*. The loop is 160 feet high. The coaster has three launches. All three go from zero to 70 in seconds. Another roller coaster first – the "top hat." On *Full Throttle* – you ride on the outside of the world record loop.

6. Not only the highest but the first as well. Six Flags Magic Mountain also has the first looping roller coaster: the *Great American Revolution*. On this coaster, you'll soar a mere 90 feet in the air.

7. The name Six Flags comes from the first park. It opened in Texas in 1961. The name is dedicated to the six nations that ruled over Texas at one time or another: Spain, Mexico, France, The Republic of Texas and The Confederate States of America.

1. A Six Flag first includes:
   a. the first tall roller coaster
   b. the largest funnel cake
   c. the first looping roller coaster
   d. the first roller coaster

2. Six Flag Magic Mountain is
   a. in Texas
   b. in Valencia, California
   c. not known for roller coasters
   d. has 120 rides

3. Six Flags is home to
   a. 800 rides
   b. 120 rides
   c. 800 roller coasters
   d. the best funnel cakes in the world

4. *Full Throttle*, in Magic Mountain, has
   a. three launches and the worlds tallest loop
   b. two launches and the worlds tallest loop
   c. two launches and a "top hat"
   d. the world's first roller coaster loop

5. Write the main idea of the reading in complete sentences.

   _____

   _____

   _____

   _____

   _____

   _____

   _____

Name: _____

Six Flags

Six Flags is a company that runs amusement parks. Six Flags was established in 1961.	15
Today, it is the largest theme park owner on earth. Six Flags has 19 parks. The parks	32
are in the U.S., Mexico, and Canada. The parks are not for the faint of heart. Six Flags	50
facts:	51

1. Six Flags sells over 15,000 funnel cakes daily. Fifteen thousand! Everyday! — 61

2. Six Flags owns over 800 rides. One hundred twenty of them are roller coasters. — 75
   Many of the highest and fastest roller coasters in the world are owned by Six — 90
   Flags. — 91

3. Six Flags Magic Mountain is in Valencia, California. It is the Roller Coaster Capitol — 105
   of the World. Home to 18 roller coasters – Magic Mountain has more coasters than — 119
   any other park on earth. — 124

4. More than 24 million people visit Six Flags parks each year. — 135

5. Six Flags Magic Mountain is home to the world's tallest and fastest looping — 148
   coaster. The coaster is called *Full Throttle*. The loop is 160 feet high. The coaster — 163
   has three launches. All three go from zero to 70 in seconds. Another roller coaster — 178
   first – the "top hat." On *Full Throttle* – you ride on the outside of the world record — 194
   loop. — 195

6. Not only the highest but the first as well. Six Flags Magic Mountain also has the — 211
   first looping roller coaster: the *Great American Revolution*. On this coaster, you'll — 223
   soar a mere 90 feet in the air. — 231

7. The name Six Flags comes from the first park. It opened in Texas in 1961. The — 247
   name is dedicated to the six nations that ruled over Texas at one time or another: — 263
   Spain, Mexico, France, The Republic of Texas and The Confederate States of — 275
   America. — 276

Words Read:	Words Read:	Words Read:
minus mistakes:	minus mistakes:	minus mistakes:
equals wpms:	equals wpms:	equals wpms:

Name: _____

Wakeboarding

Wakeboarding is a water surface sport. It is like waterskiing, only it isn't. Wakeboarding involves riding a board over the surface of a body of water. Wakeboarding was created from a combination of water skiing, snowboarding, and surfing.

To wakeboard, a rider is towed behind a boat. The boats travel at speeds of 17 to 24 miles per hour. The speed depends on the water conditions and the size of the rider. Wakeboarders ride and jump the wake made by the boat. It sounds simple, but it really isn't.

Wakeboarding was first practiced in the 1980s. The concept of "wakeboarding" was introduced by Paul Frasser. Frasser also named the sport. Paul and his brother Murray, that is. Murray was a professional snowboarder. Paul was a water skier. They combined the sports, added in a bit of surfing, and before long – wakeboarding was a thing.

The first wakeboarding competition was part of X Games II under the name World Skiboarding. Later, the World Skiboard Association changed its name to the World Wakeboard Association (WWA).

Wakeboards are made to float easily. They have fins and straps to attach the rider to the board. Wakeboarders cut across the wake of waves made by the boat towing the rider.

Wakeboarding is one of the newest sports to be considered for the Olympics. It was to appear, along with eight other new sports, in 2020; however, the 2020 Olympic games were postponed due to the Covid-19 pandemic.

Have you ever tried wakeboarding?

1. Wakeboarding is a combination of
   a. skiing, surfing and sailing
   b. surfing, snowboarding. and wind-surfing
   c. snowboarding, surfing and sailing
   d. water skiing, snowboarding, and surfing

2. Wakeboarding began in
   a. 1982
   b. 1980s
   c. Olympic competition
   d. the second X Games

3. Wakeboarding was to appear in the 2020 Olympics – why didn't it?
   a. the Olympics were cancelled due to Covid-19
   b. Paul Frasser was injured, and all decided it was too dangerous
   c. there weren't enough wakeboards
   d. the boats were too fast

4. Wakeboards are made
   a. out of the same materials as surfboards
   b. to float
   c. to jump wakes
   d. just like waterskies

5. Write the main idea of the reading in complete sentences.

   _____

   _____

   _____

   _____

   _____

   _____

Wakeboarding

Wakeboarding is a water surface sport. It is like waterskiing, only it isn't.	13
Wakeboarding involves riding a board over the surface of a body of water.	26
Wakeboarding was created from a combination of water skiing, snowboarding, and	37
surfing.	38
To wakeboard, a rider is towed behind a boat. The boats travel at speeds of 17 to	55
24 miles per hour. The speed depends on the water conditions and the size of the rider.	72
Wakeboarders ride and jump the wake made by the boat. It sounds simple, but it	87
really isn't.	89
Wakeboarding was first practiced in the 1980s. The concept of "wakeboarding"	100
was introduced by Paul Frasser. Frasser also named the sport. Paul and his brother	114
Murray, that is. Murray was a professional snowboarder. Paul was a water skier. They	128
combined the sports, added in a bit of surfing, and before long – wakeboarding was a	143
thing.	144
The first wakeboarding competition was part of X Games II under the name World	158
Skiboarding. Later, the World Skiboard Association changed its name to the World	170
Wakeboard Association (WWA).	173
Wakeboards are made to float easily. They have fins and straps to attach the rider	188
to the board. Wakeboarders cut across the wake of waves made by the boat towing	203
the rider.	205
Wakeboarding is one of the newest sports to be considered for the Olympics. It was	220
to appear, along with eight other new sports, in 2020; however, the 2020 Olympic	234
games were postponed due to the Covid-19 pandemic.	243
Have you ever tried wakeboarding?	248

Words Read:	Words Read:	Words Read:
minus mistakes:	minus mistakes:	minus mistakes:
equals wpms:	equals wpms:	equals wpms:

Where the Wild Things Are

Where the Wild Things Are was written in 1963 by Maurice Sendak. To date, the book has sold over 19 million copies worldwide. It has won a Caldecott Medal and was voted as *"one of the most distinguished American picture books for children."*

In 2012, for the 16th time, Where the Wild Thinks Are was voted the number one picture book of the *School Library Journal*.

The story only has 338 words. The book is about a boy named Max. He runs wild through his house and is sent to bed without his supper. His room turns into a magical forest. He sails to an island, tames the **wild things**, and is crowned king. Max gets lonely and returns home. And in his room – his supper is waiting for him – and it's still hot.

Fun Facts:

1. The book was originally titled Where the Wild Horses Are. Sendak, who is a self-taught artist, found out he couldn't draw horses. Maurice's partner at the time asked him what he could draw. Maurice replied, "things."

2. Where the Wild Things Are is about Sendak's childhood. Sendak says he didn't try to write for children, he wrote about himself. Where the Wild Things Are is based on Sendak's experiences as a child.

3. Where the Wild Things Are – what does it mean? It is about survival. It is about how kids can overcome anything. How they can grow and be strong. Where the Wild Things Are is about how art helps children through rage and disappointment.

Where the Wild Things Are – is it a favorite of yours?

1. Where the Wild Things Are was voted _____ sixteen times.
   a. Caldecott Medal winner
   b. number one picture book of *School Library Journal*
   c. best book of Brooklyn
   d. self-taught artist winner

2. Max returns home and what is waiting
   a. his mother
   b. his supper
   c. the wild things
   d. an empty room

3. Where the Wild Things Are is really about
   a. a wild little boy
   b. a little boy who loves his mother
   c. wild things who what to make friends
   d. the author's childhood

4. Where does Max sail?
   a. to a jungle
   b. to his bedroom
   c. to an island
   d. to the kitchen

5. On the island, Max is
   a. eaten
   b. crowned king
   c. given supper
   d. a wild horse

6. Summarize the reading in two sentences.

Name: _____

Where the Wild Things Are

Where the Wild Things Are was written in 1963 by Maurice Sendak. To date, the	15
book has sold over 19 million copies worldwide. It has won a Caldecott Medal and was	31
voted as *"one of the most distinguished American picture books for children."*	43
In 2012, for the 16th time, Where the Wild Thinks Are was voted the number one	59
picture book of the *School Library Journal.*	66
The story only has 338 words. The book is about a boy named Max. He runs wild	83
through his house and is sent to bed without his supper. His room turns into a magical	100
forest. He sails to an island, tames the wild things, and is crowned king. Max gets	116
lonely and returns home. And in his room – his supper is waiting for him – and it's still	133
hot.	134
Fun Facts:	136
1. The book was originally titled Where the Wild Horses Are. Sendak, who is a self-	151
taught artist, found out he couldn't draw horses. Maurice's partner at the time	164
asked him what he could draw. Maurice replied, "things."	173
2. Where the Wild Things Are is about Sendak's childhood. Sendak says he didn't	186
try to write for children, he wrote about himself. Where the Wild Things Are is	201
based on Sendak's experiences as a child.	208
3. Where the Wild Things Are – what does it mean? It is about survival. It is about	224
how kids can overcome anything. How they can grow and be strong. Where the	238
Wild Things Are is about how art helps children through rage and disappointment.	251
Where the Wild Things Are – is it a favorite of yours?	262

Words Read:	Words Read:	Words Read:
minus mistakes:	minus mistakes:	minus mistakes:
equals wpms:	equals wpms:	equals wpms:

Random Facts

1. The author of <u>Goodnight Moon</u> was Margaret Wise Brown. She died at 42. How? She was showing her doctor how healthy she was. She kicked up her leg. The movement dislodged a blood clot. The blood clot travelled to her heart and killed her.

2. Some people insist the moon landing was a fake. Experts agree that, in 1969, faking the moon landing would have been much harder than actually traveling to the moon.

3. In the 1890s, the train that ran between New York City and the city of Buffalo traveled one hour faster than the train that runs today.

4. A Roman soldier once farted. His fart caused a riot. Ten thousand people died.

5. A 2002 study found that the sun produces more energy in an hour than humans can use in a year.

6. McDonald's once made bubblegum-flavored broccoli. It did not go over very well.

7. There is only one letter that doesn't appear in any U.S. state name. There is no q in any state name.

8. Samsung knows people put their phones in their back pockets, so they created robots shaped like rear ends to make sure their phones can handle the pressure.

9. The blue whale is the largest animal on earth. It can weight up to 150 tons and measure 90 feet long. To move blood through its huge body its heart must beat powerfully. Its heart beats so powerfully that it can be heard two miles away.

---

1. Use the **Random Facts** to write a paragraph.

Name: _____

Random Facts

1. The author of <u>Goodnight Moon</u> was Margaret Wise Brown. She died at 42. How?	14
She was showing her doctor how healthy she was. She kicked up her leg. The	29
movement dislodged a blood clot. The blood clot travelled to her heart and killed	43
her.	44
2. Some people insist the moon landing was a fake. Experts agree that, in 1969,	58
faking the moon landing would have been much harder than actually traveling to	71
the moon.	73
3. In the 1890s, the train that ran between New York City and the city of Buffalo	89
traveled one hour faster than the train that runs today.	99
4. A Roman soldier once farted. His fart caused a riot. Ten thousand people died.	113
5. A 2002 study found that the sun produces more energy in an hour than humans can	129
use in a year.	133
6. McDonald's once made bubblegum-flavored broccoli. It did not go over very well.	146
7. There is only one letter that doesn't appear in any U.S. state name. There is no q in	164
any state name.	167
8. Samsung knows people put their phones in their back pockets, so they created	170
robots shaped like rear ends to make sure their phones can handle the pressure.	184
9. The blue whale is the largest animal on earth. It can weight up to 150 tons and	201
measure 90 feet long. To move blood through its huge body its heart must beat	216
powerfully. Its heart beats so powerfully that it can be heard two miles away.	230

Words Read:	Words Read:	Words Read:
minus mistakes:	minus mistakes:	minus mistakes:
equals wpms:	equals wpms:	equals wpms:

Name: _____

Sky Brown Skateboarder

Sky Brown was born in 2008. She was born in Japan. Sky surfs. She dances. She also skateboards.

Sky skateboards for Great Britain. She began skateboarding in 2016. She was only ten-years-old. This made her the youngest in the world.

In 2016, Sky won the world finals. She was in the 2020 Olympics and won a bronze metal. Sky skated for Great Britain. She could have skated for Japan. It was her choice. How would you like two countries fighting over you to represent them? In 2024, Sky got bronze again.

So, get this: Sky doesn't even have a coach. How does she learn new tricks? Sky watches YouTube.

Sky is sponsored by Nike. She is the youngest athlete Nike's ever sponsored. Sky is also the youngest British athlete in an Olympic games – ever.

Sky is small, but she is tough. She is also a champion.

1. Sky Brown skated in the 2020 Olympics for
   a. Japan
   b. Great Britain
   c. Japan and Great Britain
   d. the United States

2. Sky began her skating career in
   a. 2020
   b. 2016
   c. 2008
   d. 2017

3. How does does Sky Brown learn new tricks?
   a. her coach
   b. her sister and brother
   c. Instagram
   d. YouTube

4. Describe what you think a day in the life of Sky Brown would be like.

   _____
   _____
   _____
   _____

5. What is the main idea of the reading?

   _____
   _____
   _____
   _____
   _____

Sky Brown Skateboarder

Sky Brown was born in 2008. She was born in Japan. Sky surfs. She dances. She	16
also skateboards.	18
Sky skateboards for Great Britain. She began skateboarding in 2016. She was only	31
ten-years-old. This made her the youngest in the world.	42
In 2016, Sky won the world finals. She was in the 2020 Olympics and won a bronze	59
metal. Sky skated for Great Britain. She could have skated for Japan. It was her	74
choice. How would you like two countries fighting over you to represent them? In	88
2024, Sky got bronze again.	93
So, get this: Sky doesn't even have a coach. How does she learn new tricks? Sky	109
watches YouTube.	112
Sky is sponsored by Nike. She is the youngest athlete Nike's ever sponsored. Sky is	127
also the youngest British athlete in an Olympic games – ever.	137
Sky is small, but she is tough. She is also a champion.	149

Words Read:	Words Read:	Words Read:
minus mistakes:	minus mistakes:	minus mistakes:
equals wpms:	equals wpms:	equals wpms:

Name: _____

Apple Watch

First, there was the iPod. And Apple changed music. Then, there was the iPad. Books and games with a swipe. Then, the apps. All of the apps. And the iPhone. So many iPhones doing so many things.

Now a watch. But I guess it was a matter of time. It was a matter of time to have a phone in a watch. A phone in a watch and so much more! A phone, a coach, the internet, maps, books – and any app you like.

(I wrote it twice. I wrote just a matter of time twice. Do you get it? Do you get it – "matter of time?" Time…watch…anyway.)

The Apple Watch is next level connection. It is your adults with you all the time. It is social media with a swipe. It is texts on your arm!

It is Dick Tracy level. Who is Dick Tracy? He's a detective. He's a detective who basically had an Apple Watch. In the 1930s.

Google him. If you have an Apple Watch - google with Dick Tracy.

If you don't have one you want one? I do.

1. What is the order in which Apple products appear in the article?
   a. watch, iPad, iPod, iPhone
   b. iPhone, iPad, iPod
   c. iPod, iPad, iPhone, watch
   d. iPod, watch, iPhone

2. What does the reading say was only a "matter of time?"
   a. music in a watch
   b. apps to download
   c. social media on your arm
   d. a phone in a watch

3. Who is Dick Tracy
   a. inventor of the iPod
   b. inventor of the Apple Watch
   c. a 1950s detective
   d. a 1930s detective

4. What does the reading mean by "next level connection?

_____

_____

_____

5. Describe an Apple Watch.

_____

_____

_____

_____

_____

Apple Watch

First, there was the iPod. And Apple changed music. Then, there was the iPad.	14
Books and games with a swipe. Then, the apps. All of the apps. And the iPhone. So	30
many iPhones doing so many things.	36
Now a watch. But I guess it was a matter of time. It was a matter of time to have	56
a phone in a watch. A phone in a watch and so much more! A phone, a coach, the	75
internet, maps, books – and any app you like.	83
(I wrote it twice. I wrote just a matter of time twice. Do you get it? Do you get it –	103
"matter of time?" Time…watch…anyway.)	109
The Apple Watch is next level connection. It is your adults with you all the time. It	126
is social media with a swipe. It is texts on your arm!	138
It is Dick Tracy level. Who is Dick Tracy? He's a detective. He's a detective who	154
basically had an Apple Watch. In the 1930s.	162
Google him. If you have an Apple Watch - google with Dick Tracy.	174
If you don't have one you want one? I do.	184

Words Read:	Words Read:	Words Read:
minus mistakes:	minus mistakes:	minus mistakes:
equals wpms:	equals wpms:	equals wpms:

Name: _____

Busch Gardens - Williamsburg – Rides, Rides, Rides

In the summer it is hot. In the winter it is cold. That does not stop the crowds. Busch (like bush) Gardens is a theme park. It's in Virginia. It's on many lists. It is on many lists as one of the best theme park in the world.

Busch Gardens, Williamsburg has a lot to do. Roller coasters top the list. There is a dive coaster without a floor. It drops 205 feet at once. It goes up again and drops. It twists and corkscrews. It is a thrill ride not for the weak.

Apollo's Chariot spins, twists, turns, and drops 210 feet. It is a "hyper coaster." The seats make you feel like you are flying. The coaster goes 73 miles per hour. Now, that's fast.

How about going upside down? Do you like it? If so, try Tempesto. On this coaster, you'll face turns at 63 mph and inversions at 153 feet in the air. An inversion is when you go upside down.

Yes, the park has many coasters. So, if you like thrills – you'll love Busch Gardens.

1. Which coaster's drop-feet is listed?
   a. Apollo's Chariot
   b. Upside Diver
   c. Tempesto
   d. Inversion

2. An inversion is when
   a. you drop on a coaster
   b. you spin on a coaster
   c. you twist on a coaster
   d. you go upside-down on a coaster

3. Where is Busch Gardens located?
   a. California
   b. Virginia
   c. North Dakota
   d. Savannah

4. What happens during an *inversion*?

5. Describe how people feel when they are riding Apollo's Chariot.

Busch Gardens – Williamsburg – Rides, Rides, Rides

In the summer it is hot. In the winter it is cold. That does not stop the crowds.	18
Busch (like bush) Gardens is a theme park. It's in Virginia. It's on many lists. It is on	36
many lists as one of the best theme park in the world.	48
Busch Gardens, Williamsburg has a lot to do. Roller coasters top the list. There is a	64
dive coaster without a floor. It drops 205 feet at once. It goes up again and drops. It	82
twists and corkscrews. It is a thrill ride not for the weak.	94
Apollo's Chariot spins, twists, turns, and drops 210 feet. It is a "hyper coaster." The	109
seats make you feel like you are flying. The coaster goes 73 miles per hour. Now,	125
that's fast.	127
How about going upside down? Do you like it? If so, try Tempesto. On this coaster,	143
you'll face turns at 63 mph and inversions at 153 feet in the air. An inversion is when	161
you go upside down.	165
Yes, the park has many coasters. So, if you like thrills – you'll love Busch Gardens.	180

Words Read:	Words Read:	Words Read:
minus mistakes:	minus mistakes:	minus mistakes:
equals wpms:	equals wpms:	equals wpms:

Name: _____

Busch Gardens –
Williamsburg – Water
Country U.S.A.

From mild to wild - water parks have something for everyone. They have lazy rides. They have easy rides. They also have thrill rides. To be sure, water parks have rides for everyone.

Right next to Busch Gardens in Virginia is Water Country U.S.A. There are over 40 rides in the park. They have a lazy river. They also have roller coaster rides - water roller coaster rides. That's right. Water rides that are roller coasters.

What is the fastest ride? The Cutback Water Coaster. It is the only RocketBlast coaster on the East Coast. You sit on a 4-person raft. You go up and down hills. The hills are steep, and you are jet fueled. You fly through dark tunnels. You drop and dive! You scream through the water on a literal water coaster. Would you give it a try?

How about a mega-slide? Would you try a mega-slide. Colossal Curl swishes and swirls, then it throws riders into a tunnel. Twisting and turning to fall out into a wave-type pool. A thrill ride for sure.

Do you want to race your friends? Try the six-lane Nitro Racer. Riders race 320 feet on their tummies. Do you think you'd beat your buddies?

Water Country U.S.A - a great way to spend a hot day.

1. The Cutback Water Coaster is
   a. a lazy river
   b. a jet fueled water coaster
   c. an easy water coaster
   d. a mega slide

2. The Colossal Curl is
   a. a lazy river
   b. a jet fueled water coaster
   c. an easy water coaster
   d. a mega slide

3. On which ride can you race your friends?
   a. the lazy river
   b. Cutback Water Coaster
   c. Nitro Racer
   d. Colossal Curl

4. What can you infer about the Colossal Curl if it throws riders into a tunnel?
   a. riders are likely to get hurt
   b. at least some of the ride would be inside a tube
   c. the entire ride would be dark
   d. you would not get wet

Busch Gardens – Williamsburg – Water Country U.S.A.

From mild to wild – water parks have something for everyone. They have lazy	13
rides. They have easy rides. They also have thrill rides. To be sure, water parks have	29
rides for everyone.	32
Right next to Busch Gardens in Virginia is Water Country U.S.A. There are over 40	47
rides in the park. They have a lazy river. They also have roller coaster rides - water	63
roller coaster rides. That's right. Water rides that are roller coasters.	74
What is the fastest ride? The Cutback Water Coaster. It is the only RocketBlast	88
coaster on the East Coast. You sit on a 4-person raft. You go up and down hills. The	107
hills are steep, and you are jet fueled. You fly through dark tunnels. You drop and dive!	124
You scream through the water on a literal water coaster. Would you give it a try?	140
How about a mega-slide? Would you try a mega-slide. Colossal Curl swishes and	155
swirls, then it throws riders into a tunnel. Twisting and turning to fall out into a wave-	172
type pool. A thrill ride for sure.	179
Do you want to race your friends? Try the six-lane Nitro Racer. Riders race 320	195
feet on their tummies. Do you think you'd beat your buddies?	206
Water Country U.S.A – a great way to spend a hot day.	117

Words Read:	Words Read:	Words Read:
minus mistakes:	minus mistakes:	minus mistakes:
equals wpms:	equals wpms:	equals wpms:

Name: _____

Rhythmic Gymnastics

Dina Averina at the Tokyo Olympics 2021

You've seen Simone Biles fly across the floor. You've seen her flip across a beam. You know what Artistic Gymnastics (AG) is. Have you heard of Rhythmic Gymnastics (RG)?

RG is a beautiful sport. Gymnasts perform on the floor with hoops, balls, and ribbons. They even perform with clubs. They are strong. They are limber. They are very graceful.

Gymnasts compete alone. They also compete in teams. In the team events, gymnasts compete together. RG is mostly a female sport. Japan is trying to start an RG program for young men.

RG is not as poplar as AG in the United States. In Russa and Japan, RG is very popular. Girls start at a very young age. They often live together with their coaches. They practice 8 to 12 hours per day.

RG is not an easy sport, but it sure is fun to watch. Have you ever seen RG?

1. The two types of gymnastics listed in the reading are:
    a. rhythmic and artistic
    b. rhythm and artistic
    c. rhythmic and athletic
    d. artistic and rhythmic

2. RG is preformed on the floor with all of the following except
    a. balls
    b. clubs
    c. hoops
    d. bows

3. Which country is starting a men's RG program?
    a. Canada
    b. Russia
    c. United States
    d. Japan

4. In Russia and Japan, youth practice
    a. on Monday, Wednesday, Friday
    b. 3 to 4 hours per day
    c. before and after school
    d. 8 to 12 hours per day

5. The best way to describe RG is
    a. RG is a sport like curling
    b. RG is a dance sport
    c. RG is a gymnastic sport performed with hoops, balls and other things
    d. RG is not performed in the U.S.

6. From paragraph 3 of the reading, I can infer:
    a. RG is only a team sport.
    b. RG is only an individual sport.
    c. RG has both team and individual events.

Name: _____

Rhythmic Gymnastics

You've seen Simone Biles fly across the floor. You've seen her flip across a beam. 15

You know what Artistic Gymnastics (AG) is. Have you heard of Rhythmic Gymnastics 28

(RG)? 29

RG is a beautiful sport. Gymnasts perform on the floor with hoops, balls, and 43

ribbons. They even perform with clubs. They are strong. They are limber. They are very 58

graceful. 59

Gymnasts compete alone. They also compete in teams. In the team events, 71

gymnasts compete together. RG is mostly a female sport. Japan is trying to start an 86

RG program for young men. 91

RG is not as poplar as AG in the United States. In Russa and Japan, RG is very 109

popular. Girls start at a very young age. They often live together with their coaches. 124

They practice 8 to 12 hours per day. 132

RG is not an easy sport, but it sure is fun to watch. Have you ever seen RG? 150

Words Read:	Words Read:	Words Read:
minus mistakes:	minus mistakes:	minus mistakes:
equals wpms:	equals wpms:	equals wpms:

Name: _____

Extreme Fire Behavior

Fire is fire is fire. Except when it's not. What does that mean? Big fires, big forest fires, are not like most have ever seen.

Big fires make their own weather. Firestorms – read fire storms – are real. How do they happen?

When the air is dry and there is a lot to burn – the heat from a fire makes its own wind. This wind leads to strange weather.

Hot air rises. As it rises, empty space is left. Yes, a space of nothing. No air. Just heat. New cooler air around the space rushes in. The air causes an updraft and – woosh! A firestorm.

Look at the middle photo above. That's a fire cloud. Yes, there is smoke, but that is a fire cloud. Fire clouds form like other clouds. If they are large enough – they can even cause lightning.

Sometimes, the air rises fast. This causes a fire whirl. What's a fire whirl? A tornado! Like a wildfire isn't bad enough. There are fire tornados too!

I hope I never see a firestorm. Ever!

1. What is it called when fire makes its own weather?
    a.   a fire tornado
    b.   a fire cloud
    c.   a fire tornado
    d.   a firestorm

2. How does a firestorm begin?
    a.   dry air rises
    b.   air
    c.   hot air rises
    d.   air rushes into empty space

3. What does the middle photo show?
    a.   smoke
    b.   a volcano
    c.   a storm
    d.   a smoke cloud

4. What is another name for a fire whirl?
    a.   fire cloud
    b.   fire twirl
    c.   fire storm
    d.   tornado

5. What is left when the hot air rises?
    a.   smoke
    b.   air
    c.   weather
    d.   heat

Name: _____

Extreme Fire Behavior

Fire is fire is fire. Except when it's not. What does that mean? Big fires, big forest | 17
fires, are not like most have ever seen. | 25

Big fires make their own weather. Firestorms - read fire storms - are real. How do | 39
they happen? | 41

When the air is dry and there is a lot to burn - the heat from a fire makes its own | 61
wind. This wind leads to strange weather. | 68

Hot air rises. As it rises, empty space is left. Yes, a space of nothing. No air. Just | 86
heat. New cooler air around the space rushes in. The air causes an updraft and - | 101
woosh! A firestorm. | 104

Look at the middle photo above. That's a fire cloud. Yes, there is smoke, but that is | 121
a fire cloud. Fire clouds form like other clouds. If they are large enough - they can | 137
even cause lightning. | 140

Sometimes, the air rises fast. This causes a fire whirl. What's a fire whirl? A | 155
tornado! Like a wildfire isn't bad enough. There are fire tornados too! | 168

I hope I never see a firestorm. Ever! | 176

Words Read:	Words Read:	Words Read:
minus mistakes:	minus mistakes:	minus mistakes:
equals wpms:	equals wpms:	equals wpms:

Name: _____

True Crime – What Happened to Abbie? – Part I

It was March 1890. The air was crisp, but the sun was bright. Sophia Simoni was walking to school. She stopped at Aspen Avenue. She walked up to a little white house. She knocked. There was no answer.

"That's odd," she said to herself. She walked to the back door. "Abbie?" she called.

Sophia waited. It was the first day of 8th grade. She and Abbie had plans. They were walking to school. They had first period together.

"Abbie?" she called again. She checked the door. It was locked. It was never locked.

Sophia waited for five minutes. Then, she went to school. All day there was no Abbie.

At the end of the day, she walked home. She passed Abbie's house. The front door was wide open. A baby was crying.

She walked in. Abbie's brother was alone. Sophia picked him up. She walked into every room. No one else was there.

Sophia took the baby home. Her father went to the police. They searched for Abbie and her family, but they were never heard from again…until…

1. Who is missing?
   a. Abbie
   b. the baby
   c. mom
   d. Sophia

2. Sophia waited
   a. inside the house
   b. at the door
   c. at the back door
   d. at home

3. The _____ was never locked.
   a. house.
   b. door.
   c. window.
   d. baby's room.

4. Who is the baby?
   a. Sophia's son.
   b. Abbie's son.
   c. Abbie's brother.
   d. Sophia's brother.

5. Where did Sophia take the baby?
   a. to school
   b. home
   c. to the police
   d. no where

6. Abbie's house was
   a. vacant
   b. white
   c. green
   d. gone

Name: _____

True Crime – What Happened to Abbie – Part I

It was March 1890. The air was crisp, but the sun was bright. Sophia Simoni was	16
walking to school. She stopped at Aspen Avenue. She walked up to a little white house.	32
She knocked. There was no answer.	38
"That's odd," she said to herself. She walked to the back door. "Abbie?" she called.	53
Sophia waited. It was the first day of 8th grade. She and Abbie had plans. They	69
were walking to school. They had first period together.	78
"Abbie?" she called again. She checked the door. It was locked. It was never	92
locked.	93
Sophia waited for five minutes. Then, she went to school. All day there was no	109
Abbie.	110
At the end of the day, she walked home. She passed Abbie's house. The front door	126
was wide open. A baby was crying.	133
She walked in. Abbie's brother was alone. Sophia picked him up. She walked into	147
every room. No one else was there.	154
Sophia took the baby home. Her father went to the police. They searched for	168
Abbie and her family, but they were never heard from again…until…	180

Words Read:	Words Read:	Words Read:
minus mistakes:	minus mistakes:	minus mistakes:
equals wpms:	equals wpms:	equals wpms:

True Crime – What Happened to Abbie? – Part 2

The year was 1902. Sophie Simoni walked past the white house. She walked past the white house of her friend. Her best friend. The one who disappeared twelve years before.

Sophie was coming back. She was coming back to South San Francisco. She'd spent 10 years in L.A. Now, she was married. She was moving home.

She stopped at the white house. Joe, her husband, looked at her.

"What is it?" he asked.

"I had a friend," Sophie said. "She lived there. One day she was gone."

"To where?" Joe asked.

"Don't know. Nobody does. We were to walk to school one day. I knocked on her door. No one was home. Her baby brother was there. He was all alone. No one heard from the rest of her family again. The house has been empty ever since.

A shade lifted in the house. Sophie up to the window. A little girl stood inside. "Joe?" she asked.

"I see her."

"It's Abbie." Sophie ran inside. The house was empty. She looked at Joe.

"I saw her too." Joe looked around. "Let's go."

The white house burned down that night.

Sophia lived until 1996, but never saw Abbie again.

1. How many years did Sophia spend in LA?
   a. 5
   b. 10
   c. 15
   d. 20

2. Who visited the house with Sophia in 1902?
   a. Abbie
   b. Abbie's baby brother
   c. Joe
   d. Sophia's father

3. The house had been _____ since the day Sophia found Abbie's ___.
   a. empty, sister
   b. empty, brother
   c. occupied, house empty
   d. occupied, family

4. What did Abbie and Joe see in the house?
   a. a girl
   b. a boy
   c. a door open
   d. Abbie's brother

5. What happened the the house that night?
   a. Abbie moved back
   b. a family moved in
   c. nothing
   d. there was a fire

6. From paragraph 2 I can infer
   a. Abbie loved LA
   b. Abbie was excited to move home
   c. Abbie was moving back home with her husband

True Crime – What Happened to Abbie – Part II

The year was 1902. Sophie Simoni walked past the white house. She walked past	14
the white house of her friend. Her best friend. The one who disappeared twelve years	29
before.	30
Sophie was coming back. She was coming back to South San Francisco. She'd	43
spent 10 years in L.A. Now, she was married. She was moving home.	56
She stopped at the white house. Joe, her husband, looked at her.	68
"What is it?" he asked.	73
"I had a friend," Sophie said. "She lived there. One day she was gone."	87
"To where?" Joe asked.	91
"Don't know. Nobody does. We were to walk to school one day. I knocked on her	107
door. No one was home. Her baby brother was there. He was all alone. No one heard	124
from the rest of her family again. The house has been empty ever since.	138
A shade lifted in the house. Sophie up to the window. A little girl stood inside.	154
"Joe?" she asked.	157
"I see her."	160
"It's Abbie." Sophie ran inside. The house was empty. She looked at Joe.	173
"I saw her too." Joe looked around. "Let's go."	182
The white house burned down that night.	189
Sophia lived until 1996, but never saw Abbie again.	198

Words Read:	Words Read:	Words Read:
minus mistakes:	minus mistakes:	minus mistakes:
equals wpms:	equals wpms:	equals wpms:

Name: _____

This story first appeared in an August 1895 issue of the Oakland Tribune.

Chinese Kidnapping

In 1895, Xu Ming was 10. She lived in Oakland, CA. She lived with her mom and dad. They had been in the U.S. less than a year.

One day two men came to her town. They were well-dressed. Xu's mom worked in a kitchen. The men went to the kitchen each day. They ate lunch at the kitchen. They ate dinner at the kitchen. They sat at a table where they could watch Xu. They sat at a table where they could watch Xu play.

One day, the men passed Xu. They gave her candy. The next day they brought a girl with them. The girl spoke Chinese. She told Xu a fairy tale.

Two days later, Xu was gone.

Her mom and dad looked and looked for her. Their family helped. Their friends helped.

One day, Xu's dad found her in a factory. It was a shirt-making factory. The men kidnapped her and many other young girls. They forced the girls to work in the factory for free. The girls ate one meal a day. They worked 16 hours a day. They slept on the floor.

The men were arrested. They were not charged. The Chinese were not treated well in the U.S. back then. No one really cared about what happened to them.

Xu's family was upset. They worked hard. In two years, they saved enough money to go back to China.

1. Where was Xu forced to work?
    a. a kitchen.
    b. a laundry.
    c. a store.
    d. a factory.

2. Who found Xu?
    a. her mom
    b. her dad
    c. the police
    d. a social worker

3. The other girl told Xu
    a. a story.
    b. how to run away.
    c. how to sew.
    d. all of the above.

4. What can you infer about how Zu was treated?
    a. she was treated well
    b. she was treated poorly
    c. she was treated better than when she was home
    d. she liked the way she was treated

5. What is the meaning of the passage?
    a. the Chinese were treated well in the U.S. in the 1890s
    b. the Chinese were not treated well in the U.S. in the 1890s

Name: _____

Chinese Kidnapping

In 1895, Xu Ming was 10. She lived in Oakland, CA. She lived with her mom and	17
dad. They had been in the U.S. less than a year.	28
One day two men came to her town. They were well-dressed. Xu's mom worked in	44
a kitchen. The men went to the kitchen each day. They ate lunch at the kitchen. They	61
ate dinner at the kitchen. They sat at a table where they could watch Xu. They sat at a	80
table where they could watch Xu play.	87
One day, the men passed Xu. They gave her candy. The next day they brought a	103
girl with them. The girl spoke Chinese. She told Xu a fairy tale.	116
Two days later, Xu was gone.	122
Her mom and dad looked and looked for her. Their family helped. Their friends	136
helped.	137
One day, Xu's dad found her in a factory. It was a shirt-making factory. The men	154
kidnapped her and many other young girls. They forced the girls to work in the factory	170
for free. The girls ate one meal a day. They worked 16 hours a day. They slept on the	89
floor.	91
The men were arrested. They were not charged. The Chinese were not treated well	105
in the U.S. back then. No one really cared about what happened to them.	119
Xu's family was upset. They worked hard. In two years, they saved enough money	134
to go back to China.	139

Words Read:	Words Read:	Words Read:
minus mistakes:	minus mistakes:	minus mistakes:
equals wpms:	equals wpms:	equals wpms:

Name: _____

Snickers Candy Bar

Snickers is a candy bar. The first Snickers was made in 1930. The bar was made by the Mars family. It still is. Snickers was named after a horse owned by the Mars' family. Fast forward to today. Over $2 billion Snickers are sold each year. Everyone likes Snickers candy. It is the best-selling candy bar in the world.

The first Snickers were handmade. Peanut butter, nuts, and caramel were put on a tray. The trays were frozen. The candy was hand cut. The pieces were dipped in chocolate. People loved them.

There are over 18 kinds of Snickers bars made. The first is the basic bar. The basic bar is made of caramel, nuts and nougat. There is the peanut butter Snickers. There is the brownie Snickers. There is the almond Snickers. There is even a hazelnut Snickers. The basic Snicker bar is the best candy ever made.

1. Which statement is opinion?
   a. Snickers is the best candy ever made
   b. Snickers is a popular candy bar
   c. the original Snickers has nuts
   d. Snickers is the best-selling candy in the world

2. Who first make the Snickers candy bar?
   a. Venus
   b. the Venus' family
   c. Mars
   d. the Mars' family

3. Snickers was named after
   a. the maker's childhood nickname
   b. a child
   c. a dog
   d. a horse

4. Over ____ Snickers bars are sold each year.
   a. $2 million
   b. $2 billion
   c. $2 trillion
   d. the reading does not say

5. Which one is not listed as a type of Snickers?
   a. peanut butter
   b. caramel, nuts, and nougat
   c. red hot
   d. hazelnut

Name: _____

Snickers Candy Bar

Snickers is a candy bar. The first Snickers was made in 1930. The bar was made by	17
the Mars family. It still is. Snickers was named after a horse owned by the Mars'	33
family. Fast forward to today. Over $2 billion Snickers are sold each year. Everyone	47
likes Snickers candy. It is the best-selling candy bar in the world.	60
The first Snickers were handmade. Peanut butter, nuts, and caramel were put on a	74
tray. The trays were frozen. The candy was hand cut. The pieces were dipped in	89
chocolate. People loved them.	93
There are over 18 kinds of Snickers bars made. The first is the basic bar. The basic	110
bar is made of caramel, nuts and nougat. There is the peanut butter Snickers. There is	126
the brownie Snickers. There is the almond Snickers. There is even a hazelnut Snickers.	140
The basic Snicker bar is the best candy ever made.	150

Words Read:	Words Read:	Words Read:
minus mistakes:	minus mistakes:	minus mistakes:
equals wpms:	equals wpms:	equals wpms:

Name: _____

Sharks

Sharks have been on earth longer than dinosaurs. Their bones date back 450 million years. The first sharks had no jaws. They sure have jaws now. Over the years, sharks have changed. There are many kinds of sharks. Some look prehistoric. Some look like simple fish.

Sharks don't have bones. They have good eyesight. And they can smell well. Do you think sharks are smooth? They aren't. They look smooth, but they feel like sandpaper.

Sharks help keep the oceans clean. They eat fish that are sick. They keep disease from spreading.

White sharks can live to be 70-years-old.

Each shark has its own spot pattern. The spots are like fingerprints. Did you know white sharks are the biggest fish in the ocean? They are. And sharks – they are at the top of the food chain. So are people. The question is – who is top of the top?

1. Sharks have been on earth longer than _____.
   a. people
   b. mammals
   c. rocks
   d. dinosaurs

2. Sharks feel
   a. smooth
   b. like soap
   c. slippery
   d. like sandpaper

3. Sharks don't have
   a. bones
   b. teeth
   c. gills
   d. jaws

4. White sharks
   a. are small.
   b. like in lakes.
   c. are only in water above 70 degrees.
   d. can live to be 70-years old.

5. What were early sharks lacking?
   a. bones
   b. teeth
   c. gills
   d. jaws

Name: _____

Sharks

Sharks have been on earth longer than dinosaurs. Their bones date back 450	13
million years. The first sharks had no jaws. They sure have jaws now. Over the years,	29
sharks have changed. There are many kinds of sharks. Some look prehistoric. Some	42
look like simple fish.	46
Sharks don't have bones. They have good eyesight. And they can smell well. Do	60
you think sharks are smooth? They aren't. They look smooth, but they feel like	74
sandpaper.	75
Sharks help keep the oceans clean. They eat fish that are sick. They keep disease	90
from spreading.	92
White sharks can live to be 70-years-old.	101
Each shark has its own spot pattern. The spots are like fingerprints. Did you know	116
white sharks are the biggest fish in the ocean? They are. And sharks – they are at the	133
top of the food chain. So are people. The question is – who is top of the top?	150

Words Read:	Words Read:	Words Read:
minus mistakes:	minus mistakes:	minus mistakes:
equals wpms:	equals wpms:	equals wpms:

Name: _____

Lions

Lions are large cats. They are the second largest cats in the world. They live in open grasslands.

Lions are social animals. They live in groups. The groups are called prides. Each pride has about 30 lions. Lions are the only cats who live in groups.

Lions keep track of each other. Lions keep track of each other by roaring. Their roars can be heard up to 5 miles away.

Female lions hunt. They are smaller and move better than male lions. Lions hunt at night. When it is time to eat, male lions eat first. Then female lions eat. Lion cubs eat last.

Lions have cubs in litters of 2-3. Female cubs stay with their prides. They start hunting at about 2-years-old. Male cubs are pushed out of prides. They form prides with other male lions. When they are strong, they takeover mixed prides. A group of male lions stay in power for about three years.

Did you know lions are not very fast? Did you know lions used to live in Europe? Today lions only live in Africa and India.

1. Lions live in
    a.   jungles.
    b.   prides.
    c.   Asia.
    d.   groups of women.

2. How do lions keep track of each other?
    a.   by running
    b.   by eating
    c.   by hunting in groups
    d.   by roaring

3. _____ lions hunt.
    a.   male
    b.   young
    c.   female
    d.   old

4. Today, lions live in
    a.   Africa
    b.   India
    c.   Europe and Africa
    d.   Africa and India

5. Lions are _____ animals.
    a.   large
    b.   small
    c.   fast
    d.   social

6. A group of lions stay in power for about ____ years.
    a.   two
    b.   three
    c.   four
    d.   five

Lions

Lions are large cats. They are the second largest cats in the world. They live in open grasslands.

Lions are social animals. They live in groups. The groups are called prides. Each pride has about 30 lions. Lions are the only cats who live in groups.

Lions keep track of each other. Lions keep track of each other by roaring. Their roars can be heard up to 5 miles away.

Female lions hunt. They are smaller and move better than male lions. Lions hunt at night. When it is time to eat, male lions eat first. Then female lions eat. Lion cubs eat last.

Lions have cubs in litters of 2-3. Female cubs stay with their prides. They start hunting at about 2-years-old. Male cubs are pushed out of prides. They form prides with other male lions. When they are strong, they takeover mixed prides. A group of male lions stay in power for about three years.

Did you know lions are not very fast? Did you know lions used to live in Europe? Today lions only live in Africa and India.

| 16 |
| 18 |
| 32 |
| 46 |
| 61 |
| 70 |
| 85 |
| 103 |
| 104 |
| 119 |
| 135 |
| 150 |
| 159 |
| 176 |
| 184 |

Words Read:	Words Read:	Words Read:
minus mistakes:	minus mistakes:	minus mistakes:
equals wpms:	equals wpms:	equals wpms:

Name: _____

80s Fashion

High ponytails. Izod shirts. White vans. Puffy sleeves. Esprit. Switch watches. Guess. Ah, the 80s! And they are back.

The 80s were all about big hair. They were about bright colors. They were about puffy shirts. They were about crop tops and short skirts. How about bows, fanny packs and ripped jeans? Yes, those too.

Fashion in the 80s was a mix. It was a mix of the old and the new. The 1950s meets today. Eighties fashion was fun. It was punk. It was preppy. It was valley. It was hip hop – the OG hip hop.

Everyone cool had high top Reeboks and a Fila jacket or two. Yellow, green, pink, and lots of neon was the rage.

Spandex and leg warmers went viral. No longer just for dancers – they were everywhere. Those leggings so loved today. From the 80s. The comfy workout wear. Thank the 80s.

And the hair! Mullets and lots of hairspray. Hair was spiked. Ponytails were to the side. Curls and waves were all the rage.

Fashion in the 80s was fun and free. Give it a try. Throw on some neon. Slip on those vans! And rock that mullet. The 80s are back baby!

1. Which fashion brand is not listed?
   a. Esprit
   b. Izod
   c. Guess
   d. Sideout

2. _____ and _____ went viral.
   a. spandex and reeboks.
   b. Izod and reeboks.
   c. spandex and leg warmers.
   d. leg warmers and big hair.

3. Which color is not listed in the reading?
   a. yellow
   b. blue
   c. pink
   d. green

4. What is listed after bows and fanny packs?
   a. ripped jeans.
   b. Izod shirts.
   c. Guess brand clothing.
   d. Swatch watches.

5. Hairstyles in the 80s included
   a. mullets
   b. bobs
   c. side ponytails
   d. curls

80s Fashion

High ponytails. Izod shirts. White vans. Puffy sleeves. Esprit. Switch watches.	11
Guess. Ah, the 80s! And they are back.	19
The 80s were all about big hair. They were about bright colors. They were about	33
puffy shirts. They were about crop tops and short skirts. How about bows, fanny packs	48
and ripped jeans? Yes, those too.	54
Fashion in the 80s was a mix. It was a mix of the old and the new. The 1950s meets	74
today. Eighties fashion was fun. It was punk. It was preppy. It was valley. It was hip	91
hop – the OG hip hop.	96
Everyone cool had high top Reeboks and a Fila jacket or two. Yellow, green, pink,	111
and lots of neon was the rage.	118
Spandex and leg warmers went viral. No longer just for dancers – they were	131
everywhere. Those leggings so loved today. From the 80s. The comfy workout wear.	144
Thank the 80s.	147
And the hair! Mullets and lots of hairspray. Hair was spiked. Ponytails were to the	162
side. Curls and waves were all the rage.	170
Fashion in the 80s was fun and free. Give it a try. Throw on some neon. Slip on	188
those vans! And rock that mullet. The 80s are back baby!	199

Words Read:	Words Read:	Words Read:
minus mistakes:	minus mistakes:	minus mistakes:
equals wpms:	equals wpms:	equals wpms:

Name: _____

Jesse James

You've heard of Jesse James. But what do you know about Jesse James? Jesse James was a bank and train robber. In his youth, he was a "bushwhacker." Bushwhackers worked in Missouri during the Civil War. They were pro-South. The bushwhackers tortured Union soldiers. They raided houses. They did not follow any rules of war. Jesse was a great bushwhacker.

The war ended. Jesse and his brother formed a gang. They robbed banks. They robbed trains. But Jesse also got married. He had children. In his town, he was liked. He was proper. No one knew what he really did. He walked around being like everyone else.

When he robbed, he was not nice. He was brutal. Oddly, people liked him. The public liked him. They liked him as a bank robber. The gang ran from 1866 to 1876. They hit a bank in 1876. Things went very wrong. In that hit, they lost much of their gang.

Jesse was shot and killed in 1882 by a new member of his own gang.

1. During the Civil War Jesse James was a ____.
   a.   soldier
   b.   bushwhacker
   c.   robbed banks
   d.   killed

2. What did Jesse James do when the war ended?
   a.   formed a gang
   b.   became a bushwhacker
   c.   became pro-north
   d.   became a preacher

3. Which one of the following was one thing Jesse James did not do?
   a.   rob banks
   b.   rob trains
   c.   form a gang
   d.   kill his gang

4. What went terribly wrong?
   a.   a train robbery
   b.   a train robbery in 1876
   c.   a bank robbery in 1876
   d.   people in his town found out who he was

5. Where did bushwhackers work?
   a.   Missouri
   b.   Montana
   c.   Florida
   d.   the Carolinas

Jesse James

You've heard of Jesse James. But what do you know about Jesse James? Jesse | 14
James was a bank and train robber. In his youth, he was a "bushwhacker." | 28
Bushwhackers worked in Missouri during the Civil War. They were pro-South. The | 41
bushwhackers tortured Union soldiers. They raided houses. They did not follow any | 53
rules of war. Jesse was a great bushwhacker. | 61

The war ended. Jesse and his brother formed a gang. They robbed banks. They | 75
robbed trains. But Jesse also got married. He had children. In his town, he was liked. | 91
He was proper. No one knew what he really did. He walked around being like everyone | 107
else. | 108

When he robbed, he was not nice. He was brutal. Oddly, people liked him. The | 123
public liked him. They liked him as a bank robber. The gang ran from 1866 to 1876. | 140
They hit a bank in 1876. Things went very wrong. In that hit, they lost much of their | 158
gang. | 159

Jesse was shot and killed in 1882 by a new member of his own gang. | 174

Words Read:	Words Read:	Words Read:
minus mistakes:	minus mistakes:	minus mistakes:
equals wpms:	equals wpms:	equals wpms:

Name: _____

Outlaw – Sam Bass

Sam Bass was an outlaw who struck gold. Literally.

In 1877, Bass robbed a train. It was a Union Pacific train. It was carrying gold. It was carrying a lot of gold. The take was $60,000. That is $1.2 million in today's money.

After the robbery, Sam went back to Texas. He formed another gang. He was a wanted man. He was wanted by the Texas Rangers. And they found him. They found him in Round Rock, Texas.

It was a hot July day in 1878. Bass was looking for his next hit. He went into a store. A deputy sheriff was there. The deputy saw Sam. Slowly, he walked up to the outlaw.

The deputy asked for Sam's gun. Sam shot the man point blank. Sam put a bullet into the deputy.

Bass ran. The Rangers shot. Bass was hit. He died.

The thing is – the deputy didn't know it was Sam. The deputy just thought Sam looked odd. He was just going to talk to him. In fact, no one in Round Rock had ever seen Sam.

The outlaw gave himself away. Some say the gold is still hidden in Texas. You up for a treasure hunting trip?

The Train Robbers—Who Sam Bass Really was.

[From the Omaha Bee.]

The right name of Bass was not ascertained until the bodies of the two robbers were brought for burial to Ellis, a small place of not more than two hundred inhabitants. Of course the arrival there of the dead bandits created intense excitement, and everybody viewed the faces of the deceased as they "lay in state" in their coffins. Among the number who paid their respects to the thieves was a Mrs. Jacobs, who upon seeing the face of Bass exclaimed, "He was my husband," and stated that his right name was William Potts, and that he had a tattoo on the right hand, between the thumb and first finger, and a figure of a dancing girl on the right arm. The lid of the coffin was raised and his hand and arm examined, and, sure enough, the marks were found according to Mrs. Jacobs' statement.

Mrs. Jacobs was formerly the wife of a man named Jacobs, who was for a time recorder of deeds at Wichita, Kansas, and who died a drunkard. His widow afterward married Potts, but when she learned that he had a wife in Pennsylvania she left him. She had not seen him for eighteen months, and neither knew the whereabouts of the other.

William Potts

The Hays City Sentinel Hays, Kansas 19 Oct 1877, Fri • Page 1

Directions: Skim the newspaper clipping. Summarize the article and clipping in five sentences.

Outlaw Sam Bass

Sam Bass was an outlaw who struck gold. Literally.	09
In 1877, Bass robbed a train. It was a Union Pacific train. It was carrying gold. It	26
was carrying a lot of gold. The take was $60,000. That is $1.2 million in today's money.	43
After the robbery, Sam went back to Texas. He formed another gang. He was a	58
wanted man. He was wanted by the Texas Rangers. And they found him. They found	73
him in Round Rock, Texas.	78
It was a hot July day in 1878. Bass was looking for his next hit. He went into a	97
store. A deputy sheriff was there. The deputy saw Sam. Slowly, he walked up to the	113
outlaw.	114
The deputy asked for Sam's gun. Sam shot the man point blank. Sam put a bullet	130
into the deputy.	133
Bass ran. The Rangers shot. Bass was hit. He died.	143
The thing is – the deputy didn't know it was Sam. The deputy just thought Sam	158
looked odd. He was just going to talk to him. In fact, no one in Round Rock had ever	177
seen Sam.	179
The outlaw gave himself away. Some say the gold is still hidden in Texas. You up	195
for a treasure hunting trip?	200

Words Read:	Words Read:	Words Read:
minus mistakes:	minus mistakes:	minus mistakes:
equals wpms:	equals wpms:	equals wpms:

Jack-the-Ripper: Serial Killer

The year was 1888. The London streets were not safe. A man was lurking. He was killing woman. He was cutting their throats. He was taking out their organs. He was Jack the Ripper.

Jack was brutal, and he got a lot of press. The papers wrote about him. And he wrote to the papers.

This clipping is from 1888. In it, Jack is taunting the police. Jack writes: *Do you think you can catch me? Here I am. I'm at City Road. I'm telling you the place. You have to find the number. You have to find my flat number. Oh, and I plan to kill again tonight. The murder will be in Whitechapel.*

The police never found him. Alive - that is - the police never found him alive.

Jack killed over five women. He sent fear and rage through London. One day, the killings stopped. So did the letters. About a month later, a body was found floating in a river. It was Jack the Ripper. It is believed he committed suicide.

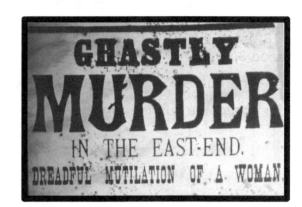

1. How did Jack the Ripper die?
    a. he was shot
    b. he killed himself
    c. he accidently drowned
    d. he was killed by a victim

2. In the clipping, Jack is
    a. taunting the police
    b. giving away his location.
    c. telling all where he will kill next.
    d. all the above.

3. According to the reading, Jack killed
    a. five women
    b. over five women
    c. men and women in London
    d. in City Park

4. Jack killed people by
    a. choking them
    b. cutting their throats
    c. hanging
    d. stabbing

Jack-the-Ripper: Serial Killer

The year was 1888. The London streets were not safe. A man was lurking. He was	16
killing woman. He was cutting their throats. He was taking out their organs. He was	31
Jack the Ripper.	34
Jack was brutal, and he got a lot of press. The papers wrote about him. And he	51
wrote to the papers.	55
This clipping is from 1888. In it, Jack is taunting the police. Jack writes: *Do you*	71
think you can catch me? Here I am. I'm at City Road. I'm telling you the place. You	89
have to find the number. You have to find my flat number. Oh, and I plan to kill again	108
tonight. The murder will be in Whitechapel.	115
The police never found him. Alive – that is – the police never found him alive.	129
Jack killed over five women. He sent fear and rage through London. One day, the	144
killings stopped. So did the letters. About a month later, a body was found floating in a	161
river. It was Jack the Ripper. It is believed he committed suicide.	173

Words Read:	Words Read:	Words Read:
minus mistakes:	minus mistakes:	minus mistakes:
equals wpms:	equals wpms:	equals wpms:

The Panama Canal

The Panama Canal is a short cut from the Atlantic to the Pacific Ocean. It opened in 1914, but it really isn't a canal. It is three sets of "locks." The locks lift boats up and down. The locks carry and push ships through Panama.

The canal took 10 years to build. Over 25,000 people died building it. Over 14,000 ships use the canal each year. The canal makes over $2 billion in tolls per year.

The French started to build the canal in 1881. So many people died of yellow fever that they gave up. A cure for yellow fever was found. The US took over. The canal was built.

The Panama Canal is 51 miles long. It is 300 feet wide. It is about 120 feet deep. It takes a third of the time to sail from East to West than before it was built. This makes trade easier. This makes goods cheaper.

Part of the canal is below sea level. That is why the ships use locks to travel from east to west.

A lock is like a big room. The room is made of cement. There are doors on both ends. The room fills with water. A ship goes in. The door closes. The second door opens. The ship moves to another lock. Water comes in, and the process repeats.

The canal has three sets of locks. It is very busy. Did you know you can take a trip through the locks? That would be fun!

---

1. How many sets of locks does the canal have?
   a. 1
   b. 2
   c. 3
   d. 4

2. What does the Panama Canal connect?
   a. north to south
   b. the Atlantic and Pacific oceans
   c. Europe to the US west coast
   d. none of the above

3. Why did the French stop building the Panama canal?
   a. yellow fever killed many of their workers
   b. they ran out of money
   c. the work was too hard
   d. they didn't have the right equipment

4. The canal is _____ miles long, _____ feet wide, and _____ feet deep
   a. 120, 51, 300
   b. 51, 120, 300
   c. 51, 300, 120
   d. 300, 120, 151

5. What is a lock in reference to the Panama Canal?
   a. something used to secure a door
   b. a cement room where ships stay dry
   c. a cement room that fills with water so ships can pass through it
   d. a type of river
   e. a tugboat used to carry people across the Panama Canal

Name: _____

The Panama Canal

The Panama Canal is a short cut from the Atlantic to the Pacific Ocean. It opened	16
in 1914, but it really isn't a canal. It is three sets of "locks." The locks lift boats up and	36
down. The locks carry and push ships through Panama.	45
The canal took 10 years to build. Over 25,000 people died building it. Over 14,000	60
ships use the canal each year. The canal makes over $2 billion in tolls per year.	76
The French started to build the canal in 1881. So many people died of yellow fever	92
that they gave up. A cure for yellow fever was found. The US took over. The canal was	110
built.	111
The Panama Canal is 51 miles long. It is 300 feet wide. It is about 120 feet deep. It	130
takes a third of the time to sail from East to West than before it was built. This makes	149
trade easier. This makes goods cheaper.	155
Part of the canal is below sea level. That is why the ships use locks to travel from	173
east to west.	176
A lock is like a big room. The room is made of cement. There are doors on both	194
ends. The room fills with water. A ship goes in. The door closes. The second door opens.	211
The ship moves to another lock. Water comes in, and the process repeats.	224
The canal has three sets of locks. It is very busy. Did you know you can take a trip	243
through the locks? That would be fun!	250

Words Read:	Words Read:	Words Read:
minus mistakes:	minus mistakes:	minus mistakes:
equals wpms:	equals wpms:	equals wpms:

Name: _____

Rap

Rap music is not new. Its roots are in Africa. Rap goes back to native tribal music. In the 1400s, slaves brought the music to the west. The music changed over time. The core stayed the same, but the music changed.

Slaves changed rhythms. They made up new rhythms from music they remembered.

About 500 years later, rap popped up in New York. A group of teens began talking in rhyme. They spoke to beats.

This was in the 1970s. Rhythms were mixed with poems. At that time, rap was street art. Kids stood on street corners. They rapped for each other. They rapped for people going by.

Rap quickly moved to clubs. It grew. It took off in September 1979. It was then that "Rapper's Delight" was released by the Sugarhill Gang. Record companies loved it. Rap exploded.

Soon rap music was popular around the world.

Jeff Pinilla - Run DMC: Streets of New York (CC License 3.0)

1. Rap traces its roots to
   a. New York City
   b. Sugarhill Gang
   c. slaves in America
   d. tribal Africa

2. Rap became popular in New York
   a. 500 years after it arrived in America
   b. in 1400
   c. in 1979
   d. on street corners

3. The first modern popular rap song released was
   a. Sugarhill Gang
   b. Rapper's Delight
   c. tribal music
   d. short lived

4. Who started modern rap?
   a. clubs
   b. a group of teens
   c. African tribes
   d. slaves

5. What is the main or central idea of the reading?
   a. the origins of rap music
   b. rap on the streets of New York
   c. rap music is not new
   d. rap music is a new form of music

Rap

Rap music is not new. Its roots are in Africa. Rap goes back to native tribal music. 17
In the 1400s, slaves brought the music to the west. The music changed over time. The 33
core stayed the same, but the music changed. 41

Slaves changed rhythms. They made up new rhythms from music they 52
remembered. 53

About 500 years later, rap popped up in New York. A group of teens began talking 69
in rhyme. They spoke to beats. 75

This was in the 1970s. Rhythms were mixed with poems. At that time, rap was 90
street art. Kids stood on street corners. They rapped for each other. They rapped for 105
people going by. 108

Rap quickly moved to clubs. It grew. It took off in September 1979. It was then 124
that "Rapper's Delight" was released by the Sugarhill Gang. Record companies loved 136
it. Rap exploded. 139

Soon rap music was popular around the world. 147

Words Read:	Words Read:	Words Read:
minus mistakes:	minus mistakes:	minus mistakes:
equals wpms:	equals wpms:	equals wpms:

Name: _____

Mars

Mars is the fourth plant from the sun. It is called the red planet. It looks red at night. Mars is the second smallest planet in our solar system. One year on Mars takes 687 days. That's a long year. A day on Mars is 24 hours and 37 minutes.

Mars has volcanos. It has plains. It has ruts. It has what look like empty riverbeds. Mars has two moons. It has seasons just like earth. And two poles just like earth.

What have we found on Mars? Lots of rocks. And in 2018 - water. Long ago there were rivers on Mars. There were lakes. We see these in the craters the water left. Now the water is in small pockets. What secrets does this water contain?

Above, Mars south polar cap. Below, Mars comparison to earth. Public domain.

The article above is not well written. It lacks transitions. It lacks flair. Please re-write it to make it better.

Mars

Mars is the fourth plant from the sun. It is called the red planet. It looks red at   18
night. Mars is the second smallest planet in our solar system. One year on Mars takes   34
687 days. That's a long year. A day on Mars is 24 hours and 37 minutes.   50

Mars has volcanos. It has plains. It has ruts. It has what look like empty riverbeds.   66
Mars has two moons. It has seasons just like earth. And two poles just like earth.   82

What have we found on Mars? Lots of rocks. And in 2018 - water. Long ago there   98
were rivers on Mars. There were lakes. We see these in the craters the water left. Now   115
the water is in small pockets. What secrets does this water contain?   127

Words Read:	Words Read:	Words Read:
minus mistakes:	minus mistakes:	minus mistakes:
equals wpms:	equals wpms:	equals wpms:

Name: _____

Title: "Extreme Fire"

First Paragraph: California is on fire. Wildfires rage through the state. Years of not taking care of the forests is taking its toll. Dryer than normal weather and no rain mean fires explode out of control. Taking better care of our forests is the only way to save our trees.

- Inferences have you read between the lines.
- Inferences have you use your own thoughts, knowledge base and ideas.
- Inferences help you figure out what the author is saying.

From the first paragraph, pictures and title, I can infer:

Use the middle photo to write the next paragraph in the article.

Name: _____

Informational Text Reader Response

THREE FACTS FROM THE READINGS:

1. _____

2. _____

3. _____

The Most Interesting Thing I Learned

_____

_____

_____

_____

_____

_____

_____

What I Would Like to Know More About

_____

_____

_____

_____

_____

_____

_____

My opinion about the article "Busch Gardens: Rides, Rides, Rides."

Answers

Hamzah the Fantastic TikTok Star: Page 9: 1. d; 2. d; 3. c; 4 a.

Billie Eilish: 1.a; 2. b; 3. c. 4. c

Kinds of Popular: 1.a; 2. c; 3. c; 4. c

Six Flags Magic Mountain: 1.a; 2. c; 3. c; 4. c

Soccer's Cristiano Ronaldo: 1.c; 2. b; 3. c; 4. a; 5. b

Sadie Sink -- Actress: 1. b; 2. a; 3. d; 4. c

My Bucket List: 1.c; 2. b; 3. d; 4. b. 5. Answers will vary.

YouTube Videos: 1.b; 2.a; 3.c; 4.a; 5. Answers will vary.

The Cell Phone Revolution: 1.b; 2. b; 3. d; 4. b.

Fantasy Football: 1.d; 2. c; 3. c; 4. **Answers should be something similar to:** Fantasy Football is an imaginary league. People draft players from different teams. Offensive players are drafted or selected individually, while defensive and special team are drafted as a whole. Drafts are like NFL drafts. The object is to draft a great team, score weekly points and make it to the postseason.

Not Your Parents' Video Game: 1. c; 2. d; 3. c; 4.c

Things to Do Before College: 1. d; 2. d; 3. a; 4.d

National Skateboarding Day: 1. c; 2. a; 3.a; 4. a.

Skateboarding Heroes: 1. c; 2. d; 3.a; 4. a. 5. Answers will vary.

National Pizza Day: 1. d; 2. c; 3.c; 4. c. 5. Answers will vary.

Music: 1. a; 2. c; 3.b; 4. d. 5. Answers will vary.

Rapper Young Thug: 1. b; 2. c; 3.c; 4. d. 5. Answers will vary.

Kanye West: 1. b; 2. a; 3.a; 4. a. 5. Answers will vary.

Cardi B.: 1. d; 2. b; 3.c; 4. b. 5. Answers will vary.

Emma Watson: 1. c; 2. b; 3.b; 4. b. 5. Answers will vary.

The Notch: 1. b; 2. d; 3. b; 4. c. The main idea of the reading is to describe the first version of Minecraft.

Sheila Johnson: 1. c; 2. b; 3 a. 4. b. The main idea of the passage is that Sheila Johnson is an ultra-successful woman and the first African American woman to have a net worth of over a billion dollars.

Sophia Bush: 1. b; 2. c; 3.a; 4. b. 5. The main idea of the passage is to explain Sophia's theories on being rich vs. making money.

Chadwick Boseman: 1. d; 2. c; 3. c; 4. c. 5. The main idea of the passage is to summarize the short, but artistic, life of Chadwick Boseman.

Black Panther (Marvel Comics): 1. b; 2. b; 3. c; 4. b. 5. Who is the Black Panther, how he was conceived, and how his life as a character progressed.

Spider-Man: 1. a; 2. b; 3. c; 4. b. 5. The main idea of the reading is to describe how Spider-man came to be.

Katniss Everdeen: 1. c; 2; b; 3; d; 4. c; 5. The main idea of the passage is to describe how strong, brave and tenacious the fictional protagonist of *The Hunger Games* book series.

Veronica Roth: 1. c; 2. c; 3. d; 4. c; 5. The main idea of the reading is to tell how Veronica Roth's Divergent book series is a smashing success.

Danny Duncan: 1. c; 2. a; 3. b; 4. a; 5. The main idea is that Danny Duncan is a YouTube star who makes a bit of money as an influencer but what's to be an actor.

Emma Chamberlain: 1. a; 2. b; 3. c; 4. a; 5. The main idea of the reading is rise and life of influencer Emma Chamberlain.

Nike: 1. c; 2. a; 3. a; 4. b. 5. The main idea of the passage is the Nike Air Force 1 is a popular shoe and one of the first to be in such demand that it was reissued.

LeBron James; 1.b; 2.d; 3. a; 4. b; 5. The main idea is that Lebron James is an amazing athlete and one of the best basketball players ever to play the sport.

Joan of Arc – Part 1: d; 2. d. 3. c; 4. a 5. The main idea of the passage is to summarize the life and legacy of Joan of Arc.

Joan of Arc – Part 2: 1. b; 2. d; 3. d; 4. a; 5. Joan of Arc was a brave military leader for France who was captured by the English, they looked for anything to punish her. Ultimately, she was put to death because she dressed like a man.

Wonder Woman: 1.d; 2. b; 3. d; 4. b. 5. The main idea of the reading is to tell about Wonder Woman over the years, especially the early years.

Magic the Gathering: 1. c; 2. b; 3. c; 4. d; 5. Magic the Gathering is the most popular trading card game ever and one that can bring you lots of money. If you collect the right cards.

Six Flags: 1. c; 2. b; 3. a; 4. a 5. The main idea of the passage is to inform the reader about the daring and amazing roller

Answers

coasters within the world of Six Flags.

Wakeboarding: 1. d; 2. b; 3. a; 4. b; 5. The main idea of the passage is to tell the history of wakeboarding.

Where the Wild Things Are: 1. b; 2. b; 3. d; 4 c.

Sky Brown: 1. b; 2. b; 3. d; 4. Answers will vary; 5. The main idea of the reading is to tell about a young Japanese, British skateboarder named Sky Brown.

Apple Watch: 1. c; 2.d; 3. d. 4. Next level connection means that the Apple Watch brings people closer than ever. We had technology before, but this is way more. 5. The apple watch is a phone and a coach and the internet and maps and books and so much more – right at on your wrist.

Busch Gardens: 1. a; 2. d; 3. b. 4. You go upside down; 5. When people ride Apollo's Chariot, they fell like they are flying. They may be frightened. They go 73 miles per hour. They feel twisty and turny.

Busch Gardens Water Country: 1. b; 2. d; 3. c; 4. b

Rhythmic Gymnastics: 1. a; 2; d; 3; d; 4 d; 5; c; 5; c

Extreme Fire Behavior: 1. a; 2. c; 3. d 4. d 5. d

True Crime: What Happened to Abbie: Part 1: 1. a; 2. c; 3. b; 4. c; 5 b; 6. b.

True Crime: What Happened to Abbie: Part 2: 1. b; 2. c; 3. b; 4. a; 5. d; 6. c

Chinese Kidnapping; 1. d; 2. b; 3. a; 4. b; 5. b

Snickers Candy Bar: 1. a; 2. d; 3. d; 4. b; 5. c

Sharks: 1. d; 2. d; 3. a; 4. d. 5. d

Lions: 1. b; 2. d; 3. c; 4. d; 5. d; 6. b

80s Fashion; 1. d; 2. c; 3. b; 4. a; 5. b

Title: "Extreme Fire": From the title and the photographs, I can infer that the author believes that the causes of the wildfires in California are the result of dry weather and forests that are not taken care of.

Jesse James: 1. b; 2. a; 3. d; 4. c; 5. a.

Jack the Ripper: Serial Killer: 1. b; 2. d; 3. b; 4. b

The Panama Canal: 1. b; 2. b; 3. a. 4. c; 5. b

Rap: 1. d; 2. c; 3. b; 4. c; 5. a

Fluency Tracker

Name: _____ Period: _____

Passage #	Date	CWPM	Date	CWPM	Date	CWPM

Fluency Chart

Name: _____   Period: _____

Correct Words Per Minute																									
115																									
110																									
105																									
100																									
95																									
90																									
85																									
80																									
75																									
70																									
65																									
60																									
55																									
50																									
45																									
40																									
35																									
30																									
25																									
20																									
15																									
10																									
5																									
Date																									
Passage Title																									

Made in United States
Troutdale, OR
11/20/2024

25084174R00077